52 Activities for Improving Cross-Cultural Communication

52 Activities for Improving Cross-Cultural Communication

**Donna M. Stringer
and Patricia A. Cassiday**

INTERCULTURAL PRESS
A Nicholas Brealey Publishing Company

BOSTON • LONDON

First published by Intercultural Press, an imprint of Nicholas Brealey
Publishing, in 2009.

Nicholas Brealey Publishing
20 Park Plaza, Suite 1115A
Boston, MA 02116, USA
Tel: + 617-523-3801
Fax: + 617-523-3708
www.interculturalpress.com

Nicholas Brealey Publishing
3-5 Spafield Street, Clerkenwell
London, EC1R 4QB, UK
Tel: +44-(0)-207-239-0360
Fax: +44-(0)-207-239-0370
www.nicholasbrealey.com

© 2009 by Donna M. Stringer and Patricia A. Cassiday

Printed in the United States of America

13 12 11 10 09   1 2 3 4 5

ISBN: 978-1-931930-83-3

Library of Congress Cataloging-in-Publication Data Applied for

Contents

Activities

Appendices

Acknowledgments

This book is made possible by the many colleagues who have contributed exercises and who have kindly offered editorial suggestions that have improved our own exercises. Our colleagues, Andy Reynolds and Elmer Dixon at Executive Diversity Services, Inc. in Seattle, have been particularly generous in developing, testing, and improving communication style exercises. Faculty at the Summer Institute for Intercultural Communication in Portland, Oregon, have contributed substantially to our thinking and skills as trainers and educators, with a special thanks to Janet Bennett. And the rich resource of books offered by Intercultural Press has been our foundation.

We thank the editorial and production team at Intercultural Press for their expertise and careful editing. We owe our enthusiasm for, and confidence in, an experiential learning approach to Sivasailam Thiagarajan, "Thiagi," and Dianne Hofner Saphiere, to whom we are grateful. Thiagi is a master of the experiential approach, and he always encourages his students to find their own answers to the question. And Dianne has designed many experiential approaches to learning, including the Cultural Detective series, which we have used to the benefit of our clients and participants.

We hope this book is useful to you. Please modify the activities to meet the needs of your audience—as we have through the years.

The authors have made every effort to cite and acknowledge all those from whom research, lecture material, or activities have been adapted.

Introduction

The problem with communication … is the illusion that it has been accomplished.

George Bernard Shaw

Culture

In order to consider cross-cultural communication, it is necessary to understand some basic definitions. Culture can be seen as a system of thinking and acting that is taught by, and reinforced by, a group of people. Cultural groups teach their members certain sets of values, with accompanying behaviors and communication preferences. Haslett (1989) argues that we learn culture and communication simultaneously, very early in life. This tacit "cultural understanding" of the world then influences our personal preference in communication style and continues to influence our perception of others throughout our life.

Defining culture as a systematic way of thinking and behaving within a group requires that we think of culture beyond any simple groupings of nationality, ethnicity, or gender. Organizations are known to have their own "culture" that influences the way "we do business." Orienting new employees to an organization's culture so they know how to "behave properly" and participate effectively in the organization can be a key factor in that employee's success. (Schein 1985).

Cross-Cultural Communication

Cross-cultural communication, then, is that which occurs between people who may have different cultural perspectives. This can include the entire range of differences from nationality to age to different departments within the same organization.

The exercises in this book are intended to facilitate effective communication across a wide range of differences. Many of the exercises are written with instructions that address needs for a specific audience (e.g., gender or generation). We encourage you, the user, to adapt the exercises to fit the needs of the particular audience with whom you are working.

It will also be important to *prepare your audience* for receptivity by reviewing two issues prior to using the exercises in this book:

1. *Generalizations vs. Stereotypes.* We know that communication styles are patterns that people learn from the range of cultures in which they have membership. A "generalization" or "cultural norm" is the pattern of communication used by the majority of people in any cultural group. It is equally true to say that every culture has a "communication style norm" that is used by a majority of people in that culture and to say that a cultural norm is not likely to apply to every individual within the culture. In other words, cultural norms can apply to most people in a group but do not apply to every individual in the group. When a cultural norm is applied to everyone in a group in a rigid manner, we have shifted from generalizations to stereotypes (Bennett 1998). Cautioning your participants about this will likely reduce their unconscious tendency to stereotype; and it is likely to reduce the resistance some participants will exhibit when they think you, the facilitator, have just stereotyped a group.

2. *Perception* is also highly susceptible to both personal and cultural experiences. Consequently, doing a very brief exercise to demonstrate perception differences can be a "fun" way to help people understand how extremely different communication styles can lead to negative perceptions about another person.

Cross-Cultural Miscommunication

LaRay Barna (1997) has identified six primary sources of cross-cultural miscommunication:

1. *Assumption of similarities.* The "invisible" aspects of our culture lead us to assume our communication style and way of behaving is how "everyone" communicates and behaves. When they act "like us" we think they are right or we don't give it much thought. When someone acts differently, we may judge them negatively.

2. *Language differences.* Speaking a non-native language can easily lead to miscommunication. Even people speaking the same language can experience miscommunication because the same word can mean something very different. For example, "pop" on the west coast of the United States usually means a soda drink, while on the east coast it often refers to drug use or

shooting someone; being "stuffed" in the United States generally means you have had too much to eat, while in Australia it often means you are pregnant. These are differences that can have serious miscommunication impacts.

3. *Nonverbal misinterpretations.* We send and receive wordless messages through body language, facial expression, and eye contact. Even clothing and furniture style can communicate an intended or unintended message.

4. *Preconceptions and stereotypes.* Culture influences the way we see the world. Preconceived notions and stereotyping occur when "oversimplified" characteristics are used to judge a group of people or an individual associated with a group.

5. *Tendency to evaluate.* When we hear communication or observe behavior, we tend to interpret the message or the action through our cultural lens. We may evaluate the message or behavior as "good" or "bad" without really understanding the intent.

6. *High anxiety.* Not understanding what is appropriate or expected can raise our anxiety level. Miscommunication can be a direct result of being in an anxious state.

We have incorporated exercises throughout this book that are aimed at exploring each of these barriers to effective communication.

Some Great Techniques

One can find "tools" or "techniques" for improving communication in many books in the fields of cross-cultural communication, international business, and communication among others. We urge facilitators to go beyond the specific objectives in any single exercise and provide participants some specific techniques for improving cross-cultural communication as a takeaway from their workshops or classes. We have incorporated techniques in exercises throughout this book and suggest creating a handout of your own that lists your favorite techniques and provides participants something tangible to practice as they communicate across the widest range of cultural differences. Our favorite list is found in Appendix A on page 229. Feel free to use it and/or modify it to fit your audience.

Why This Manual?

Many publications offer a variety of exercises for exploring cross-cultural differences. This book is unique in its singular focus on cross-cultural communication exercises. As educators and trainers attempt to teach about cross-cultural communication, having a single source for such experiential activities makes the search for relevant experiences much easier.

We have collected and adapted existing communication activities from many sources. We have developed and contributed a large number of our own exercises to this book. No matter what your situation, we hope you will find an appropriate exercise to meet your objectives.

Who Is This Manual For?

As intercultural trainers and educators, we have used each of these activities in corporate or educational environments throughout the world. We have used them in higher education and high school settings. Most of these exercises are designed for adult learners, however, so use with younger participants may require some adaptations.

If you are an instructor of students for whom English is a second or foreign language (ESL/EFL) you will find many activities here to help your students gain insight into their own communication and how to be more effective with others. You may also want to allow more time than allotted for each activity.

One exercise that we use frequently and find extremely useful for examining second language acquisition is called Redundancia. This exercise is not included in this book because it requires a specific handout and is copyrighted by Nipporica Associates. We urge you to consider purchasing it through *www.nipporica.com*.

Organizational leaders, military personnel, missionaries, and students preparing to study abroad will benefit from understanding cross-cultural communication in order to create greater effectiveness. In short, anyone who is interested in becoming more effective in communication with others will find much of value in these pages.

What Will You Get from This Manual?

You will find not only a wide variety of activities on communication but also two mechanisms (see "How to Use This Manual" on page xiii) for helping you choose the right activity for your situation. Each activity includes all that you need to conduct it:

1. *Time Required* to conduct the activity, broken down according to each segment of the exercise.
2. *Objectives* for the activity in an easy-to-read list that can be shared with participants.
3. *Materials required.*
4. *Process* with clear, numbered instructions for conducting the exercise.
5. *Debriefing Questions* that will help you assist participants in identifying what they have just learned. Note that we have purposely written these questions to be fairly general because

we have found that asking a few germane questions generates rich discussion and meaningful learning.

6. *Debriefing Conclusions* identifying basic learning points we hope will be identified by the participants during the activity and the debriefing. These are for you, the facilitator, to use as a conclusion with the hope that the participants have already identified them.

7. *Additional Processes.* In some activities, we use multiple ways of conducting an exercise. Where this is true, we have given you those alternatives.

You will also find a General Classification of Activities (Appendix B) at the end of the book that summarizes information about each activity. The classifications are intended to help you make quick decisions about which of the activities you want to use. The list of References (Appendix C) concludes the book with readings on cross-cultural communication styles and theory. These additional materials can be helpful in deepening your own understanding of cross-cultural communication.

How to Use This Manual

Choosing the right activities for your particular audience can be a time-consuming task—time that you would far rather spend preparing for an activity than searching for one. To help you with the important task of selecting an exercise, we have supplied a chart (Appendix B on page 231) called "General Classification of Activities." Reviewing this chart before flipping through the exercises can help you save time and assist you in choosing the most appropriate activity for your group. Once you have identified several exercises that might fit your needs, you can then review them to select the one(s) you will use. This chart categorizes all 52 activities by Context and Type of Communication; Communication Themes; Risk Level, and Time Required.

Context and Type These activities are adapted by Context: Workplace and Education and by Type: Verbal, Nonverbal or Written Communication.

Communication Themes include Conflict, Decision Making, Negotiation, Gender, Gestures, Greetings, Ice Breaker, Second Language, Seeking to Understand, Self-Awareness, Style Differences, and Team Process. It is important to point out that virtually all of these exercises will help participants understand their own preferences and their perception of those whose communication style may be different. Participants will be encouraged to take the perspective of the other in achieving greater understanding and effectiveness. Removing the barriers of misperception and building the bridge of perspective-taking are key elements in effective communication—something that every exercise in this book seeks to enhance.

While some of these exercises *focus* primarily on interpersonal communication, others focus more on team or organizational communication issues. We have not included this category in our classifications because we believe that improving communication in one of these areas essentially affects all three areas. Facilitators will want to identify the primary focus they want to achieve as they introduce and debrief.

Risk Level It is difficult to gauge the level of risk involved in an activity because what is of medium risk for one person may be quite threatening to another. In general, however, we can assume low, low-medium, medium, medium-high, and high risk. Knowing your audience and your own skill level is important when selecting a risk level. Beginning trainers need to consider their depth of understanding and skill in handling the group process. We recommend an inexperienced trainer work with an experienced trainer when implementing high-risk activities.

Time Required Listings are in total minutes required to complete the activity, including the debriefing. We don't recommend that you try to skimp on the time allotments, especially debriefing, which is the most essential and valuable aspect of an activity to ensure learning.

Debriefing Approach

Debriefing is a critical key to learning—it guarantees that learning has occurred and that participants have not just "had a good time" with an activity. The debriefing questions are based on David Kolb's learning styles (see below). The questions explore feelings, thoughts, observations, actions, and applications for each exercise in an effort to meet the style preferences of participants.

You are welcome to add more debriefing questions if you like, but we caution less experienced trainers against using too many questions during the debriefing. Asking a few germane questions is more likely to generate rich discussion and more meaningful learning. Additionally, we caution inexperienced trainers to provide sufficient time for debriefing because, as mentioned earlier, this is where much of the learning takes place.

A Note about Adult Learning Styles

David A. Kolb's (1985) approach to learning styles served as a framework and guide for our development of these activities. Kolb discusses four types of learning preferences: (1) concrete experience,

(2) reflective observation, (3) abstract conceptualization, and (4) active experimentation. We have attempted to include as many types of learning preferences in each activity and debriefing as fit the activity conceptually. Following is a brief description and example of each type of learning preference:

1. *Concrete Experience* requires learning by relating to other people and identifying feelings. Small group discussions regarding personal experiences and feelings about an issue make use of this preference.

2. *Reflective Observation* requires people to observe what goes on around them, think about what they have seen, and explore their observations from a range of perspectives. Even though this preference is the most difficult to address in training because of the length of time it can take, it can be included through a journal writing activity or by the debriefing questions asked.

3. *Abstract Conceptualization* involves systematic planning, logical analysis, and intellectual understanding of a situation or theory. This is addressed through lectures or problem-solving activities such as case studies. This is also why it is important to precede any communication styles exercise with information about stereotyping vs. generalizations and experiences with perception differences.

4. *Active Experimentation* is the "doing" preference and includes completing self-assessment instruments and participating in simulations and role-plays, among other activities. Participants often remember active experimentation as the most enjoyable part of a class or workshop. Because people learn differently, however, "doing" cannot be the entire focus of the training. It is important for you to know that these activities can be high risk and may not be appropriate based on your participants' comfort with risk, and your own level of experience.

While many will ask, or demand, that your training design be primarily experiential—a trend in both corporate and educational settings today—we caution you to balance all four styles. Too much "doing" can result in little or no understanding of the underlying reason that a behavior or action may or may not be effective cross-culturally; too much "thinking" can result in participants being bored or not learning how to apply the information. Balance is the key to great training and effective learning.

Communication Continuum Exercise

Time Required:

60 minutes: 15 minutes for lecture and exercise instructions, 20 minutes for small group exercise, 25 minutes for debriefing

Objectives:

To help participants:

1. Identify the range of communication style preferences in the group.
2. Identify the strengths and weaknesses of both their own preferred communication style and other styles in the workplace.
3. Learn a tool for listening.
4. See the value of having, and using, all three styles.
5. Identify the cost to workplaces of expecting people to adapt rather than use their own preferred style.

Materials:

Flip chart paper, marking pens

Descriptions of communication styles in a PowerPoint slide and/or in a handout

Description of TING in a PowerPoint slide and/or in a handout

Process:

1. Prepare three flip charts with labels of Detached, Attached, and Intuitive.
2. Using the attached outline, provide participants with descriptions of three communication styles. Stress that cultural groups teach and reinforce a "preferred" style of communication and that these three styles are on a continuum. State that while individuals may use all three styles, and that the situation or context will determine which style we use, there tends to be a preferred style—one in which we are most comfortable. Ask people to identify which style is their most

comfortable style and to go to the flip chart with that label on it. (*Note: Some people will insist that they use two or all three styles. Indicate that this is likely true—and that you would like them to select the style that they would prefer to use most often if circumstances would allow. If this does not resolve the issue, ask them to go to the style they would like to spend the next 20 minutes discussing.*)

3. With the three groups you have created, ask people to respond to the following concepts. (*Note that you are now asking people to consider the context of the workplace. That is, you have asked them to identify their personal preference and now you are asking them to consider their preferred style in the context of the workplace.*) Provide each group with several marking pens. (*Note that no group should be larger than 7–8 people. If any group is too large, divide it into a second group for that style.*)
   a. The strengths and weaknesses of our style in the workplace.
   b. How *each* of the other two styles helps us and hinders us in the workplace.

4. Tell the groups to select a reporter. Give them 20 minutes to complete this task.

5. Bring the groups back together and ask that people practice good listening skills during the reporting. Teach them TING using the overhead and the attached description. Remind them that this is a good time for them to hear how others may experience their primary communication style.

6. Ask each group to place its flip chart sheets where everyone can see them. Ask the reporter from each group to share the results of their discussion: first, how they see their own strengths and weaknesses and then how each of the other styles helps and hinders them at work.

   Note: Be prepared for lots of giggling, teasing, and so forth. Continue to respectfully remind people to listen carefully and be nonjudgmental. Let the group have fun but not at one another's expense.

7. After all three groups have reported out and have their sheets posted, ask for observations and begin the debriefing.

Debriefing Questions:

1. What did you notice as you listened to each group's report? Listen for:
   a. What one group sees as its strengths, other groups often see as a weakness and vice versa.
   b. Groups tended to describe both themselves and others in much the same way.
   c. Every group brings something powerful to a team.

2. What implications does this information have for teams?
3. How will you use this information when you return to work?

Debriefing Conclusions:

1. All three styles bring value to the workplace.
2. We all tend to agree about both the strengths and weaknesses of each style. We know them all.
3. While others may see the same strengths and weaknesses in our style that we do, the tendency is for us to downplay the weakness while others may highlight it in evaluating us.
4. The greatest strength for a team is when all three styles are available to call on.
5. All three styles are effective in coming to solutions and decisions although they may come to them in different times and in different ways.
6. Most workplace cultures recognize and reward one style and ignore or actively eliminate the other styles. This leaves people for whom the least rewarded styles are their preference with two primary options: either adapt at work in order to fit in, or retain one's preferred style and be perceived and treated like an outsider. This can result in enormous loss of resources for the workplace.

Attachment: Communication Continuum Exercise

COMMUNICATION STYLES:

- Describe the three communication styles using the following descriptions.
- Ask people how those who use each style might perceive people using the other styles.

Detached Communication Style: Communication "should" be calm and impersonal. Objectivity is valued. Emotionally expressive communication is seen as immature or biased.

Attached Communication Style: Expression of feelings is an important and necessary part of communication. Subjectivity is valued. Objectivity can be seen as "not caring."

Intuitive Communication Style: Communication of global concepts or ideas is valued. There is frequent use of metaphor and expression of abstract ideas. May appear to others to deviate from the topic but intuitive communicators see the connection.

TING:

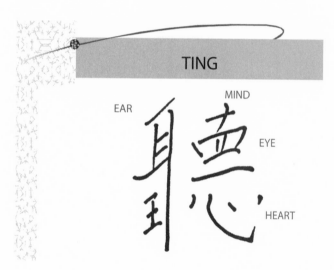

Explain that TING is the Chinese word for "To Listen." In order to listen effectively, you need to use:

- Your ear to literally hear the words
- Your mind to understand the words
- Your eye to observe nonverbal messages
- Your heart to understand the feelings of the speaker

Explain that in order to genuinely communicate with another person, it is important to listen with all four senses.

Second Language Walk-in-Their-Shoes

Time Required:

20 minutes: 5 minutes for the exercise, 15 minutes to debrief

Objective:

To assist one-language speakers to appreciate the effort that "new" second language learners and speakers exert while communicating in their nonprimary language.

Materials:

None

Process:

1. Ask participants to choose a partner and decide who will go first.
2. Facilitator gives the following instruction: "Now tell your partner about the town you grew up in. Start. OH WAIT!!! As you share this information insert a COLOR[1] every seventh word, using a different color each time. Go!"
3. After two minutes ask that they switch and the other partner do the same.

Debriefing Questions:

1. How did you feel when you were the speaker? What did you do?
2. How did you feel when you were the listener? What did you do?
3. How effective were you?
4. What did you learn?
5. How can you use this awareness as you interact with others who are speaking a second or third language?

---

[1] Use any word that makes sense to the audience (e.g., animals, foods, acronyms from their organization, products from their organization).

WORKPLACE
EDUCATION
L

Debriefing Conclusions:

1. Second-language speakers can feel awkward, can take longer to find the word they want to communicate, and may be limited in the words available to them.
2. When listening to second-language learners, the listener can get impatient and/or may try to help by giving them a word.
3. Using empathy from your own experience can increase effectiveness for both the listener and the speaker.

Adapted from an activity by Scott Horton, Delta Concepts Consulting and Training, Atlanta, GA.

Decoding "Work Speak"

Time Required:

30 Minutes: 5 minutes to introduce and give examples, 5 minutes for exercise, 20 minutes to debrief

Objectives:

1. To assist participants in understanding disconnects that happen when people assume they understand one another without clarifying work agreements.
2. To provide participants with a simple way to check those assumptions, resulting in less time lost and improved relationships and trust among colleagues.

Materials:

A PowerPoint slide or flip chart with words and categories

Process:

1. Project or present a flip chart with the following display:

> ### Your Code
>
> - Conflict Talk:
>   - *Annoyed, Irritated, Frustrated*
> - Agreement Talk:
>   - *Fine, OK, Pretty good*
> - Project Talk:
>   - *Right away, ASAP, Timely*
> - Decision Talk:
>   - *Not comfortable, Disagree, I'd do it differently*

2. Ask people to select a partner. When everyone has a partner, introduce the exercise.
3. Using the first category of "Conflict Talk" describe a situation in which two people have a conversation. Demonstrate an

WORKPLACE
VERVAL
M–H

exchange using the following script and appropriate tones for each speaker.

    a. Person A: *I'm* **irritated** *that we didn't get the project done yesterday.*

    b. Person B: *Yeah. OK, moving on—let's talk about tomorrow.*

    c. Person A: *Excuse me? I just told you I was* **irritated***!!!*

    d. Person B: *Oh, well, now it sounds like you're actually* **annoyed***!*

    e. Person A: *No! Why aren't you listening to me? If I was simply* **annoyed***, I wouldn't have even brought it up!*

    f. Person B: *Well, if you were only* **irritated** *then why is it such a big deal???*

4. Point out that the two people in this example are from the same country, the same age, the same gender, the same ethnic origin, the same educational background, and both have English as a first language. And that they *still* are having a challenging time understanding each other.

5. Ask participants to individually "rank" the three words in all four categories (Conflict, Agreement, Project, Decision) according to their own "Personal Code." Have them rank them from one to three with three being the "strongest" for them personally.

6. Give your own personal example for one part such as: *"For me, if I say I'm* **irritated** *that means I'm REALLY mad. But if I say I'm* **frustrated** *it's just a minor thing. And* **annoyed** *is somewhere in the middle."*

    (Facilitator Hints): Go through each category and tell them the following for their ranking system:

    a. Conflict: Most Mad to Least Bothered

    b. Agreement: I Like It a Lot to It's Just Acceptable

    c. Project: Right Now This Instant to When You Can Get It Done

    d. Decision: Go Ahead if You Must to Over My Dead Body, No Way!

7. Instruct the group members once they have completed their own rankings to share them with their partner and see where their "personal codes" are the same/different. Allow approximately five minutes for this discussion.

Debriefing Questions:

1. How many had 100 percent agreement/alignment with each other? If there are a few pairs that raise their hands congratulate them! And assure them that if they ever end up in a work project conflict with each other there is a high likelihood that they will actually understand what the other person is saying!

2. If you found differences between you and your partner, what was your first reaction?
3. What could be the implications of these differences for work teams?
4. What other issues might cause the same types of differences or misunderstandings? (Watch for cultural differences of any sort including ethnic, gender, generational, or language.)
5. What actions, specifically, could mitigate these potential misunderstandings? Whenever leaving a room or a discussion in which an "agreement" has been reached, check for understanding by using the following statement: *"Can you tell me what you mean by (_____)?"*

   For example, your boss said: "I need that report 'right away.'" Perhaps the boss means before the end of the day and you and your whole team should drop every other priority, or perhaps it means before the next meeting on that particular topic—which happens to be on Friday. Clarifying "right away" with one little sentence can help to save a tremendous amount of work and misunderstanding.

Debriefing Conclusions:

1. Even when speaking the same language and using the same words, individuals can interpret the strength of a word very differently.
2. Before you leave the room or the conversation, the "gap" is just in words and usually easily clarified. Once you've left and begun to act based on your assumptions, the implications of misunderstanding the other's "code" becomes much more significant—and the possibility for emotional implications becomes much greater.
3. Checking for understanding of meanings can avoid misunderstanding—and becomes even greater with each cultural difference between participants.

Adapted from an activity by Barbara Grant, MA ABS, Principal Consultant for MGS Consulting, Seattle. *www.mgs-us.com*

Alpha-Beta Partnership

4

WORKPLACE
VERBAL
NONVERBAL
M–H

Time Required:

60 minutes: 5 minutes for introduction, 15 minutes to prepare in homogeneous groups, 20 minutes to negotiate in mixed groups, 20 minutes to debrief

Objectives:

To help participants experience how:

1. Communication patterns change when cultural differences are introduced to a group.
2. Both cultural behaviors and communication patterns can impact negotiation between two groups.

Materials:

8–30 participants

Two rooms

Distribution of Rewards sheet for each participant

Alpha sheet for each participant in one group

Beta sheet for each participant in one group

Process:

1. Divide the participants into two groups, placing each group in a separate room. Give Distribution of Rewards and Alpha sheets to each participant in one room; give Distribution of Rewards and Beta sheets to each participant in the other room.
2. Each group should choose a leader according to its cultural attributes.
3. Have the groups practice their cultural behaviors separately by solving the Distribution of Rewards problem in their own group first before entering into negotiation with the other group. They will use the results of this preparation to enter negotiation with the other group.

4. After 15 minutes, take the Alpha and Beta sheets away from participants. Do not discuss the results with the groups.

5. Each group prepares to negotiate with the other group by splitting in half and sending half to meet with the other group. Therefore, one group gets to host and one group gets to visit. You can call one group the Field group and one group the Headquarter group, if you wish. You can allow Alpha-Alpha or Beta-Beta consultation during the negotiations if you choose.

6. The Alpha-Beta negotiations proceed, using Distribution of Rewards.

7. You observe the two negotiations and stop them after 20 minutes. Bring all participants together in the same room and ask each mixed group to report the results of their negotiation.

Debriefing Questions:

1. How did you feel in the homogeneous group when you were first practicing your cultural behaviors? What was your communication like with your cultural group?

2. How did you feel when you first entered the new group (either as a visitor if you were a Field representative or as a host if you were in Headquarters)? What happened to communication between your cultural members and the new group? What happened to communication between your own cultural group as a result of the new group being introduced to the room?

3. What behaviors did you notice during the negotiation? (Focus people on reporting behaviors.)

4. How did you feel about the behaviors you noticed? How did these feelings affect behaviors?

5. How did the different cultural behaviors affect the negotiation and communication?

Debriefing Conclusions:

1. We tend to be most comfortable communicating with people from our own "group" and that can include our company/department, gender, age, country, and so on.

2. When we encounter people from another "group" we may retreat and become less communicative *or* become more assertive—depending on both personality differences and differences in culturally learned appropriate behaviors.

3. Culturally learned behavioral differences affect communication behaviors, which will affect the style and outcome of negotiations.

Alphas

GREETINGS

Members do not touch each other or others. Touching strangers is considered rude and vulgar and is reserved for intimate family members. Greetings are usually a quick bow of the head "hello" and then down to business.

THE TEAM

Members believe in the power and strength of the individual. Each person has the responsibility to contribute to the team to the best of his/her ability in his/her own way.

LEADERSHIP

The leader is the person with the strongest, most dominant personality and is chosen by majority vote. The leader initially presents the team's position during negotiations.

PROBLEM SOLVING/DECISION MAKING

Problems are best solved through impersonal logic and rational argument. Decisions are reached through a vote and majority wins.

CONFLICT

Conflict is healthy and normal. In conversations, you feel free to disagree with others and encourage others to disagree with you.

Betas

GREETINGS

Members greet others by touching lightly on the shoulder. Inquiries about self and family well-being must be made before business discussions can begin.

THE TEAM

The harmony of the group is very important and each team member is very solicitous of fellow group members.

LEADERSHIP

You come from a culture in which age and experience are revered. The eldest member of the group is automatically the leader and deferred to by the rest of the group. The leader chooses the person who is to present the team's initial position in negotiations.

PROBLEM SOLVING/DECISION MAKING

Problems are best solved through consensus. Each member of the team must agree before any action may be taken.

CONFLICT

Conflict is seen as something to be avoided. Disagreement is expressed through silence and bowing of heads.

Created by Marcella Peralta Simon, adapted from an exercise of the same name by Richard Brislin.

Distribution of Rewards

The ALPHA-BETA joint venture partnership recently received a contract for $800,000 U.S. dollars to build a road in a third-world country. Given a number of fortunate circumstances, such as good weather, the project was completed for $700,000. It is now the end of the fiscal year and the board of directors has decided that the extra $100,000 can be distributed in bonuses among the people involved in the project the way financial managers at Headquarters and the line managers in the Field office (which oversaw the project) from both partner companies decide. The people involved were evenly distributed among Alphas and Betas.

Person A was the hardest worker and was clearly responsible for supervising a great deal of the actual day-to-day work on the project. At least 40 percent of the day-to-day work on the project was done by him.

Persons B, C, and D were solid but not spectacular contributors. They were competent workers but not outstanding. Each contributed about 15 percent of the actual day-to-day work on the project.

Person E is a very high-status and wealthy person in the organization and in the community. Although he did not engage in any of the day-to-day work on the road construction project and did not write the proposal for funding, it is known within the organization that he called upon his connections and used his influence so that the original $800,000 contract would go to the company.

Person F is a contributor much like B, C, and D. His contribution was about 15 percent of the work needed for the project's completion. His father died recently, however, and person F has considerable expenses associated with the funeral, nursing care for his mother, and the education of his much younger brothers (his father left no estate).

Note that the contribution of A, B, C, D, and F total 100 percent of the project's workload.

As financial managers from ALPHA and BETA companies you are meeting first with your colleagues at Headquarters or in the Field office to agree on a position and then to discuss your position with your counterparts and reach a joint partnership agreement.

Agreement in Homogeneous Group:

AMOUNT OF BONUS   REASON

    Person A

    Person B

    Person C

    Person D

    Person E

    Person F

                Total = $100,000

Agreement in Negotiation between Alphas and Betas:

AMOUNT OF BONUS   REASON

    Person A

    Person B

    Person C

    Person D

    Person E

    Person F

                Total = $100,000

5

A Fair Shake

Time Required:

20–30 minutes: 10 minute activity and 10–20 minutes to debrief

Objectives:

To help participants:

1. Experience how it feels to have your identity redefined.
2. Experience how it feels to change a "conventional" gesture like shaking hands.
3. Recognize cultural discomfort in general and comfort with physical contact specifically.

Materials:

None

Process:

1. Have everyone circulate in the room until you give a signal for them to stop and shake right hands with the nearest partner, announcing their first name and repeating what they hear. This should go on a number of times so everyone has a chance to meet.
2. Give new instructions: Think of an adjective starting with the first letter of your first name and a noun starting with the last letter of your first name (e.g., Pallid Rabbit for Peter). Demonstrate this on an easel or white board.
3. Ask participants to begin circulating again and shake left hands as they meet, exchanging their new names (the two words).

Optional:

Conduct another round of introductions, only ask participants to shake with another part of the body when meeting one another. You can specify which part of the body (e.g., elbows) or allow individuals to make their own choices.

4. Debrief.

Debriefing Questions:

1. How did you feel during the second round of introductions? Why?
2. What are the cultural issues that could arise during this exercise?
3. How did it feel to be asked to change your name? Who could this happen to in "real life"?
4. How did you feel during the third round of introductions? What went through your mind as you were asked to use a different part of your body with which to introduce yourself?
5. What cultural misperceptions could happen during the simple act of introducing ourselves? What communication techniques could be used to reduce the potential for misunderstanding?
6. What are the possible implications for ongoing communication with others once you have introduced yourselves?

Debriefing Conclusions:

1. There are many cultural ways of introducing ourselves and they have implications for how we perceive each other and communicate thereafter.
2. When people are asked to change a "natural" behavior (e.g., moving from right to left hand) it can feel very awkward and take considerable energy to remember to do it "right." Others can be advantaged and use less energy (e.g., people for whom their left hand is their dominant hand have just been given an advantage, perhaps for the first time ever).
3. When people are asked to change their identity it has emotional implications.
4. There are considerable cultural differences in the acceptability of touching: who, where, how, and so on.

Optional ways to conduct exercise:

- Depending on the language, the two words could be noun/adjective. Depending on how names are used in the culture or in the training context, the two words could correspond to the last name or the first name.
- Before debriefing, ask participants to write down as many names from the second round as they can remember. Discuss why. Notice that people are so focused on their own new name that they listen less effectively to others.
- Ask participants to explain why they chose their new name and what if anything it might have to do with their personality, their background, or their culture. This helps to introduce

the notion that culture is as much "in here" (our own cultural identity) as "out there" (the way foreigners behave).

- The facilitator can note down the names and use them later in the training for various reasons: humor, examples of creativity, to highlight cultural associations, and so on.

Caution to trainers:

This activity is not necessarily to be used with all cultures or with all groups (e.g., this activity will need to be modified for cultural effectiveness depending on the group's gender composition, hierarchical considerations, or appropriateness of physical contact). It could also be used as a predeparture exercise for people moving from a "non-contact" to a "contact" culture.

Adapted from an activity by Peter Isackson, International Communication for Business Management (ICBM), Paris, France.

The Language of Gestures

6

Time Required:

30–45 minutes: 15–20 minutes activity and 15–25 minutes for debrief

Objectives:

To help participants:

1. Discover the cultural randomness of gestures.
2. Experience the impact of using arbitrary gestures.
3. Explore dissonance when expectations are contradicted.
4. Understand the difficulty of learning new codes.
5. Illustrate the nature of "meaning" (producing action).

Materials:

Create a Gesture Handout sheet for each group that includes four different gestures. Gestures should use heads or hands and should represent greeting, invitation, approval, and rejection. Gestures should not be culturally recognizable to the group, and the same gesture should be given different meanings on different sheets.

Process:

1. Divide the group into subgroups of 4–6 participants.
2. Give each group a Gesture Handout.
3. Give participants five minutes to memorize the meaning of their four gestures: greeting, invitation, approval, rejection. (The gestures are the same for all groups but the attributed meanings will be different on handouts.)
4. Allow groups five minutes to practice appropriate standard reactions to each gesture as follows:
   Greeting = repeating the same gesture
   Invitation = coming to the side of the person inviting
   Approval = smiling and expressing joy
   Rejection = turning away and leaving

5. Create pairs from different groups and give the following instructions: "Without talking, use the four gestures to interact with the aim of agreeing to do something together." They must only use the four gestures and the standard reactions. This should produce total confusion.

6. After approximately five minutes, stop the activity and debrief the experience.

Debriefing Questions:

1. How did you feel trying to learn and practice the new gesture codes and the assigned reactions?
2. What did you think when your gesture met with an unexpected reaction?
3. What issues can arise from using common gestures from your own culture in another cultural setting?
4. What experiences have you had with unexpected reactions to a gesture? Allow people to share their information with the group.
5. What strategies or communication techniques could be used to reduce the potential for misunderstanding?

Debriefing Conclusions:

1. Gestures have arbitrary cultural meaning; the same gesture can have different meanings in different cultures and different gestures can have the same meaning.
2. Dissonance in codes lead to misperception, misunderstanding, and confusion.
3. Unexpected reaction produces surprise and sense of discomfort.
4. Learning new codes is difficult.
5. Ask about gestures within the cultural context to avoid miscommunication.

Optional way to conduct the exercise:

In step 5 each group selects a delegate to go and dialogue with a different group. Each group receives a "foreigner" who begins the dialogue with one of the group members. Others in the group are observers. The subgroup can then try to figure out what happened before the whole group debriefs.

Adapted from an activity by Peter Isackson, International Communication for Business Management (ICBM), Paris, France.

7

Rational, Emotive, Intuitive

Time Required:

60 minutes: 15 for lecture about styles, 5 to get into small groups and give instructions, 20 for small group exercise, 20 for debriefing

Objectives:

1. To identify the range of communication style preferences in the group.
2. To allow participants to identify the strengths and weaknesses of their own preferred style in the workplace.
3. To allow participants to identify the strengths and weaknesses of the other styles in the workplace.
4. To allow the group to see the value of having, and using, all three styles.
5. To identify how much stronger a team can be if people are allowed to use a preferred style of communicating rather than adapting a team norm in order to be acknowledged and rewarded.

Materials:

A copy of the Communication Style Continua and descriptions (Attachment A) for each participant.

A copy of TING for each participant (Attachment B).

An easel, paper, and marking pens for each small group (minimum of 3)—or whiteboards.

Process:

1. Give a brief lecture, defining each of the cultural communication styles on the attached list. Stress that each *row* is a continuum and that people may move back and forth, using different styles based on the setting and context for communication, but that cultures teach us the "best" way to communicate that can leave each of us with a preferred (most comfortable) way

to communicate on each continuum. Also get the group to consider how people on one end of each continuum might perceive (and/or label) those who are using the style on the other end of the continuum.

2. Stressing that communication styles are always on a continuum, and that everyone uses all three styles at some time, ask participants to create a triangle (using three points you identify in the room) with Rational, Emotive, and Intuitive spots. Allow people to place themselves between two points if they feel they use two styles equally comfortably. Ask each person to think about how they *prefer* to communicate (where they tend to begin) and stand somewhere along the lines you have designated.

3. Once people are where they feel comfortable, ask those who are in between two points to make a choice, temporarily, about which of the two styles they might be most comfortable with. In other words, get people into three groups for the purpose of the rest of the exercise. Stress that you know they will use different styles in different settings but for the next few minutes you want them to decide which style they would like to identify with.

4. Creating three groups (Rational, Emotive, Intuitive), ask each group to record the following things on flip chart paper.
   • The strengths and weaknesses of our style in the workplace.
   • How each of the other two styles helps me and hinders me in the workplace.
   Give each group three sheets of paper and several marking pens. Note: If one group is too large (e.g., Rational), split it into two. No group should be larger than 7–8 people.

5. Ask each group to select a reporter. Give them 20 minutes to complete this task as a group.

6. Bring the groups back together and ask that people practice good listening skills during the reporting. Teach them TING using Attachment B. Remind them that this is a good time for them to hear how others may experience their primary communication style.

7. Ask each group to post their flip chart pages on the wall where they can be seen by everyone. Ask them first to share how they see themselves and then how they see the other two groups. If you have more than one group for any of these styles, ask the second group to bring their sheets up and post them but only to report anything they have concluded that is different from the first group reporting.

Note: Be prepared for lots of giggling, teasing, etc. Continue to respectfully remind people to listen carefully and be nonjudgmental. Let the group have fun but not at one another's expense.

8. After all three groups have reported and have their sheets posted, ask for observations and begin the debriefing.

Debriefing Questions:

1. What did you notice when you were in your small groups?
2. What did you notice as each group reported?
3. What implications does this have for teams?

Debriefing Conclusions:

1. All three styles bring value to the workplace.
2. We tend to agree about the strengths and weaknesses of each style. We know them all.
3. While others may see the same strengths and weaknesses in our style that we do, the tendency is for us to see the strengths of our style while others may see the same behavior as a weakness.
4. The greatest strength for a team is when all three styles are available.
5. All three styles are effective in coming to solutions and decisions although they may come to them in different times and in different ways.
6. Most workplace cultures recognize and reward one primary style. The result is that those who have styles that are not the norm may adapt to fit in—and in the process use more energy adapting than being productive. And it also results in the team losing the strength of those styles that are suppressed.

Optional ways to conduct the exercise:

1. With limited time, the facilitator can select one or two of these continua and conduct the exercise without discussing all five continuum.
2. TING can be eliminated from the exercise.
3. Language can be changed to make this relevant to educational settings.

Attachment A: Communication Style Continuum

Direct _____ Indirect _____ Storytelling

Low Context _____ High Context

Faster Paced _____ Slower Paced

Formal_____ Informal

Rational_____ Emotive_____ Intuitive

While each individual may use multiple styles, there are identifiable, culturally taught preferences. Use of multiple styles is common although there tends to be a personal preference that is the style individuals may revert to under pressure. Misperceptions and/or conflict is common when individuals are using different styles. Style refers to *how* one speaks, not *what* one says.

DIRECT:

- What one means is stated in a straightforward, direct manner. No "beating around the bush."
- Directness is equated with honesty and respect for the other person and the other person's time.
- Supports the values of saving time and focusing on task.

INDIRECT:

- Meaning is conveyed by subtle means such as nonverbal behaviors, questions, stories, parables, or use of a third party.
- Indirectness is equated with politeness and respect for the other person and the other person's feelings.
- Supports the values of relationship, history, and group harmony.

STORYTELLING:

- Meaning is conveyed through stories or parables.
- Stories are equated with allowing others to decide the meaning for themselves.
- Supports the values of relationship, history, and group meaning.

LOW CONTEXT:

- The context of communication is not assumed to be known. Things must be explained clearly and unambiguously.
- Tends to use lots of words because the words establish the context/meaning.

HIGH CONTEXT:

- The context of communication is assumed to be known. It is unnecessary, even disrespectful, to explain things precisely.
- Tends to use few words because the context establishes the meaning.
- Leaves understanding to the other person and respects their understanding of the situation.

FASTER PACED:

- Speech patterns are rapid, indicating engagement and intelligence.
- Expect answers to questions immediately.
- Risk is eliminating participation by people whose culture has taught a more reflective, slower pace; those who have some forms of disability (e.g., hearing loss), and those for whom English is a second language.

SLOWER PACED:

- Speech patterns are slower, indicating reflection and thoughtfulness.
- Responses to questions expected after the other person has time to reflect; not immediate.

FORMAL:

- Communication is governed by strict rules regarding such things as forms of address based on age, status, topics.
- Communication is ritualized, including the use of organizational hierarchy to determine who can/cannot be talked to and under what circumstances.
- Supports the values of status and hierarchy.

INFORMAL:

- Communication has few rules; people tend to be addressed by first name.
- Communication is less bound to specific conventions. More flexibility in what is said, to whom one can speak, and under what circumstances.
- Supports the values of fairness and equity.

RATIONAL:

- Focus is on objective information/data and tends to be linear.
- The emphasis is on ideas that are separate from the person. Disagreement with another person's ideas is acceptable and even valued. It is not seen as a personal attack.
- Listen carefully to the ideas; if you disagree say so—the disagreement is with the idea, not the person.
- Preference in discussion is to remain objective and not personalize—indicates objectivity and fairness.
- Preference for "taking turns" when talking.
- Information generally presented in a linear manner.
- Less comfortable with feeling discussions.
- Less variation in tone or gestures.

- When announcing a decision, focuses on facts or information.
- To be effective be brief, state the point, and avoid lengthy explanations.

EMOTIVE:

- Focus is on feelings. Tends to appear more people-oriented and passionate. Communication may be more circular.
- The emphasis is on the person, so great importance is attached to feelings. Issues, ideas, and the person are not separate. Disagreement, if done at all, is done carefully and often indirectly because the person and idea are not separate—disagreement with ideas is an attack on the person.
- Sharing one's values and feelings about the issues is highly valued—indicates personal investment.
- Can overlap (interrupt) when others are speaking
- Generally can hear feeling in the voice regardless of volume.
- May present information in a more circular manner.
- The point may be left unstated because the verbal and nonverbal information is sufficient for understanding; stating the point explicitly may be seen as disrespectful.
- Prefers to involve people and aim for consensus.
- Greater variation in tone and gestures.
- When announcing a decision, may describe it in terms of how it will affect people, relationships, or morale.
- To be effective, use stories, allow time for embellishment.

INTUITIVE:

- Focus is on "knowing" based on experience. The connection between knowing and experience is often not conscious.
- Discussion is more internal with self than external with others.
- Process is less linear, and is less conscious, and more difficult to describe to others.
- Increased experience may lead to more rapid decisions although the process for getting there is neither conscious nor subject to justification.
- Prefers more reflection to identify the "knowing" than external discussion.
- When announcing a decision, typically just gives the decision without justification.

SOURCES:

Condon, J. C., and F. Yousef. (1975). *An Introduction to Intercultural Communication*. New York: MacMillan.

Kim, Y. Y. (1986). *Interethnic Communication*. Newbury Park, CA: Sage Publications.

Nelson, G. L., M. A. Batal, and E. B. Yaguida. (2002). Directness vs. indirectness: Egyptian Arabic and US English communication style. *International Journal of Intercultural Relations*, *26*, 39–57.

Saphiere, Dianne Hofner, Barbara Kappler Mikk, and Basma Ibrahim DeVries. (2005). *Communication Highwire: Leveraging the Power of Diverse Communication Style*. Yarmouth, ME: Intercultural Press.

Attachment B: TING

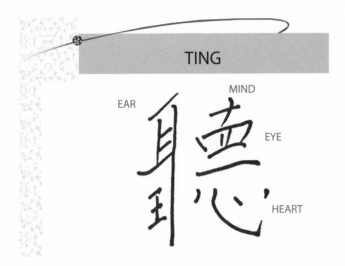

- TING is the Chinese word meaning "To Listen"—it describes a very complete way of listening so that your total focus is on the speaker. Often, when we are listening to another person, we are only partially listening while we are preparing our response. With TING, you are fully present to the speaker.
- The symbol on the left-hand side is ear—I use my ear to hear the words you are speaking. The symbol on the lower half of the left-hand side translates to "king" or "dominant one," indicating that the ear is the most important part of listening.
- On the right-hand side at the top is mind. I use my mind to understand the words you are saying. Below that is eye. I use my eye to watch for any nonverbal messages you are sending me. If the verbal and nonverbal are inconsistent, I can ask for clarification. The line below that is one, or "to become of one," indicating that we can become of one heart if I listen effectively. Heart is the bottom symbol on the right-hand side.
- In other words, if I listen to you with TING, I am fully attending to you. I have nothing left to get defensive with. No matter what you are saying, I am fully focused on you, not on me. The closest we have in English to this word is "active listening" or "empathy."
- Listening in this way will almost always result in a much deeper level of understanding than we are generally accustomed to. When we do this, relationships almost always benefit and people will feel included and engaged.

What Would You Do?

8

Time Required:

45–60 minutes: 30 minutes for activity and 30 minutes to debrief

Objectives:

1. Describe range of "appropriate" responses in a given scenario.
2. Explore the diversity of communication styles within the group.

Materials:

Post-it notes

Pen or pencil for each participant

Communication Styles Handout (distribute after step 3)

Four pieces of poster-size paper: Each with a situation

Situation 1: You have been asked to prepare a one-hour presentation. The day before the presentation, your colleague says you have just 10 minutes to present. You are frustrated about the change. What would you do?

Situation 2: One of your coworkers comes to your office frequently and interrupts your work. What would you do?

Situation 3: You are at an important social function and an acquaintance at your table makes a comment that offends you. What would you do?

Situation 4: You are at a meeting and a colleague compliments the work you have done, so much so that you feel embarrassed. What would you do?

Process:

1. Ask participants to read and decide how they would respond to each situation.
2. Have them record individual responses on Post-it notes and place them on the appropriate situation chart.
3. Ask participants to choose one charted situation to stand next to. Balance the four groups.
4. Ask each group to examine the responses to their situation.
5. Distribute the Communication Styles Handout. Review the style preferences listed on page 33.
6. Cluster responses into "style" preference.

Debriefing Questions:

1. Which style preferences were presented for your situation?
2. Was there one style that was preferred? Not present on the chart?
3. What are some advantages of the preferred style? What might be a disadvantage of that style?
4. How might the other preferences apply to this situation?
5. How might miscommunication occur if the sender and receiver have different style preferences?

Debriefing Conclusions:

1. A wide range of communication style differences exist within every culture.
2. Minor communication style differences can have major effects on interactions and relationships.

Optional ways to conduct exercise:

The situations can be varied to fit the training goals. The situations can be topic specific and designed to elicit a wide range of responses and discussion of specific topics such as teaming challenges, mergers between organizations or departments, and/or cross-cultural assignments.

Communication Styles Handout[1]

Direct: Get to the point. "Don't beat around the bush." Brevity and being linear are often rewarded.

Circular: Telling a story or providing enough information so the point "speaks for itself." A great deal of information is provided, allowing the listener to reach the conclusion on his or her own.

Indirect: Bringing up the point in such a way that the individual can "save face" and maintain positive feelings. Harmony in relationships is a higher priority than exactness or speed in communication.

Person-centered: Communication is a vehicle for building personal relationships. Verbal and nonverbal communication have the ability to enhance or damage relationships because the meaning and message are often closely integrated with the identities of the communicators.

Idea-focused: Communication around ideas involving critical thinking or passionate discussion is essential for showing commitment to the ideas and people involved. Lively debate between friends, family, or coworkers is satisfying and can positively impact relationships.

---

[1] Note: The explanations on this page were adapted with permission for *Communication Highwire* from William Gudykunst and Stella Ting-Toomey (1988), and Janet Bennett and R. Michael Paige (1996), and from training materials by Barbara Kappler Mikk and Rhonda Davey (1999).

Reprinted with slight adaptation and permission from Dianne Hofner Saphiere, Barbara Kappler Mikk, and Basma Ibrahim DeVries, *Communication Highwire: Leveraging the Power of Diverse Communication Styles*, Intercultural Press, 2005, Activity 1, pages 15–16.

How Would I Say That?

9 (top-right)

WORKPLACE
EDUCATION
VERBAL
M

Time Required:

60 minutes: 5 minute introduction, 25–30 minute activity, 25–30 minutes to debrief

Objectives:

To help participants:

1. Recognize the influence context has on communication style.
2. Explore how the goal or purpose of the communication influences style.
3. Observe ways cultural values and/or gender roles influence a communicator's style.
4. Observe how status/power roles influence communication style.

Materials:

Index cards with a "Speech Act" on the card

A Speech Act Handout for each participant

Pen/pencil and paper or index cards for participants

Process:

1. Introduce activity and give brief (5 minute) overview of "speech acts" listed on handout.
2. Divide participants into small groups (6–8). Each group draws three cards with different speech acts (e.g., "give a compliment to a coworker" etc.).
3. Ask individuals to jot down how they would personally communicate the speech act. Participants then share their response with the group.
4. Remind group members to pay special attention to diversity in responses.

5. Have participants in small groups discuss differences and commonalities, paying special attention to differences by gender, culture, age.
6. Debrief the activity with the large group to include interesting and/or surprising observations.

Debriefing Questions:

1. Which speech acts were easy? What might make the same act more difficult?
2. What differences within the group surprised you? Were you able to discuss the differences?
3. How might culture affect individual responses/expectations? Were there any generational differences in response/expectations?
4. How might gender affect some speech acts? Male/female? Female/male?
5. How did the communication change when family members were involved? Was it easier or more difficult to deal with the family members? Why or why not?
6. How did you feel when you communicated a need to a supervisor or family elder?

Debriefing Conclusions:

1. Cultural values and/or gender roles influence the way we send and receive messages.
2. Status/power roles influence communication styles.
3. Generational expectations often differ in style and expectation, especially related to age, status, and direct vs. indirect communication.
4. Although we may have preferred styles, other style choices are available.
5. "Receiver's" style is an important factor to consider.
6. Context (where/when the message is sent) influences communication style.
7. It is important to be clear about your goal or purpose for the communication.

Optional ways to conduct exercise:

Ask for volunteers to role-play the activity for the large or small groups and then debrief the "style" used to meet the communication goal.

How Would I Say That? Handout

(Sample Speech Acts)

1. Give a compliment about the clothes someone is wearing.
2. Give a compliment about a well-written memo, e-mail, or paper.
3. Request time off from work or class to attend a family funeral.
4. Request more challenging projects at work or school.
5. Use humor to lighten the mood after a stressful meeting.
6. Explain that you will not meet a deadline.
7. Request new office furniture or a change of office/dormitory.
8. Thank someone for his or her help with a project.
9. Praise a colleague for a well-run conference or event.
10. Critique a supervisor or teacher for being late to a meeting.
11. Critique a subordinate or a friend for being late to work.
12. Tell a family member you are not going to a family dinner.
13. Tell a family member you are not going to a cousin's wedding.
14. Apologize for taking a week to respond to an e-mail.
15. Apologize to a friend for forgetting you had dinner plans and you have now made another commitment.
16. Give someone feedback about how their performance could be improved.
17. Tell someone that something they said offended you.

Reprinted with slight adaptation and permission from Dianne Hofner Saphiere, Barbara Kappler Mikk, and Basma Ibrahim DeVries, *Communication Highwire: Leveraging the Power of Diverse Communication Styles*, Intercultural Press, 2005, Activity 20, pages 233–235.

10

E-mail: Communicating Across Cultures

Time Required:

60–90 minutes: 60 minutes for activity, 30 minutes for debrief

Objectives:

To help participants:

1. Observe differences in written communication style (e-mail).
2. Recognize impact of style on workplace productivity.
3. Explore style switching to influence task accomplishment.

Materials:

Paper and pencil or flip chart and markers

E-mail scenarios on 4×6 note cards (See Attachment A. These can be adapted to be culture specific or organization specific.)

Handouts: Communication Style Descriptors (See Attachment B), Guidelines for Feedback (See Attachment C)

Process:

1. Distribute and discuss the Communication Style Descriptors.
2. Explain the purpose and overall flow of the activity.
3. Place participants into small groups of 4–6 (as diverse as possible).
4. Invite one member to come up and draw a scenario card.
5. Give the group 20 minutes to read the scenario and draft an e-mail in response. (When writing the response, they should consider communication style factors and descriptors of the colleague described.)
6. Pair small groups. Each group sends their e-mail and original scenario card by server (a team member) to the other team.
7. Allow 10–20 minutes for the group to read the scenario and the e-mail written by the other group, and to write feedback for the other team following the "feedback guidelines."

8. Have the two teams meet and share their feedback verbally, attempting to learn from the other team's observations.

Debriefing Questions:

1. How did you feel at the beginning of the activity? Composing the e-mail as a group? Receiving and discussing the feedback?
2. Which communication style descriptors were most useful for your scenario?
3. What differences within the group surprised you? Were you able to discuss the differences?
4. Did the discussion of the scenarios affect an awareness of your personal communication preferences? In what way?
5. How might this activity influence your everyday work? Personal communication style?
6. What additional tips might you add to the "tip writing list"?

Debriefing Conclusions:

1. Awareness of communication style preferences can enhance communication effectiveness.
2. In written and verbal communication the intent of the sender and the impact on the receiver may not be the same.
3. Discussion of the communication goal and review of the written communication (prior to sending the message) may improve outcome.
4. All communication styles have strengths and weaknesses. Style switching can influence collaboration and increase productivity.

Attachment A: E-Mail Scenarios

1. You have a Chinese colleague, Aling, whom you have known for several years. You are currently working on a project with Aling and have been putting time and energy into the project while also balancing your other work. You have a deadline to meet on Aling's project, but it now looks as though you will not be able to meet the deadline because of some technical challenges as well as your staff's summer vacation schedule. You know that Aling will be very upset, and that she has little respect for the fact that so many of your staff take vacations at the same time. You want to reassure Aling that you are doing your best and will continue to try to meet the deadline. Please e-mail Aling to let her know. In her communication style Aling tends to value and express concern for others; social niceties, such as apologies for difficulties; a strong work ethic; and predictability and commitment.

2. You are planning a trip to Cameroon to make presentations on a new program you are introducing. Arnaud, your contact there, has worked very hard to plan your week's schedule, and has managed to make appointments for you with several high-profile people. Your boss, however, has just told you to delay your trip for one week. Please e-mail Arnaud to let him know. In his communication style, Arnaud tends to share background information and to tell stories. He expresses a concern for group welfare while trusting age, education, and experience. He values his word and his commitments. Arnaud also seems quite comfortable expressing both his positive and negative emotions.

3. Karl, one of your German international student volunteers, wrote to you that he could not come to help at an orientation as planned, but you never read that e-mail. You get back to your desk and are ready to write a very short e-mail demanding to know where he was when you realize he did send an e-mail to you. You feel that Karl's e-mail was very brief and you really do not know why he missed the orientation. You had a very hard time without him. How do you respond?

4. You have a Venezuelan colleague, Jaime, with whom you need to coordinate your work efforts. Jaime has given you several different dates for when he will be finished with his portion of the work so that you can begin, and you want to confirm the correct information. Please e-mail Jaime, to straighten this out. In his communication style Jaime tends to talk about pleasurable experiences inside and outside work. You know him to be a very proud man who sees himself as incredibly trustworthy and sincere.

5. You have been working on a joint development project with a Dutch colleague, Henk. He promised to create and get to you some drawings that you need. Henk gave himself a deadline that passed three weeks ago, and this delay is negatively influencing your work. You need to know when you can actually expect the drawings, and how you might help him to get them done more quickly. Please e-mail Henk so you can get this matter resolved. In his communication style, Henk tends to be concise and forthright. He does not use a lot of "social lubricants" and appears to appreciate honesty and explicit communication. You know that Henk hates to be told what to do, and that he approaches teamwork and decision making from a consensual orientation.

6. Your U.S. college student, Megan, sends you a long e-mail detailing why her assignment is late. In her e-mail, she discloses a lot of personal information regarding her family situation, her problems at work, her feelings about her other instructors and their lack of understanding about her situation, and confidential information about her roommate, whom you also have as a student in one of your classes. Her high level of disclosure, especially about people you know, and her explicit and open manner of communicating makes you uncomfortable. Because it is Thursday evening, and you do not have classes on Friday and will not be seeing Megan until the following week, you feel that it is important to respond via e-mail, yet you are unsure of what to say and how to say it. How would you respond to Megan's message?

Attachment B: Communication Descriptor Charts[1]

Communication Style Descriptor Checklist

DISCERNIBLE		DISCOVERABLE

DISCERNIBLE

1. Beginning & Ending a Conversation

1a. Beginning

NV/hesitant ———————————— Verbal/assertive

1b. Ending

Sudden —————|———————— Elaborate
       Clear closure

2. Presentation of Ideas

2a. Sequencing of function
___ task, ___ relationship, ___ process, ___ other

2b. Sequencing of information
___ general then specific, ___ specific then general, ___ integrated, ___ specific w/o general, ___ general w/o specific, ___ other

2c. Structure of expression
___ outline, ___ storytelling, ___ stream of consciousness, ___ zig zag, ___ other

2d. Degree of preparation

Spontaneous ———————————— Planned

2e. Links between ideas

Explicit ———————————— Implied
transitions   connections

2f. Tools of influence
___ data, ___ experience, ___ proverb/parable, ___ intuition, ___ relationship, ___ emotion, ___ other, ___ none

3. Turn Taking

3a. Timing
___ any time, ___ speaker breath,
___ listener audible breath,
___ speaker finishes, ___ listener moves,
___ at key point,
___ listener assumes speaker finishes,
___ other

3b. Style
___ bowling, ___ basketball, ___ rowing,
___ tennis, ___ other, ___ none

4. Vocal Characteristics

4a. Tone

Formal ———————————— Casual

4b. Rate

Rapid ———————————— Slow

4c. Volume

Loud ———————————— Soft

4d. Vocal sounds
Describe:

5. Nonverbal Characteristics

5a. Eye contact

Hold gaze ———————————— Look away

5b. Facial expression
Describe:

5c. Gestures
Describe:

5d. Personal distance

Inside ————|———— Outside
personal space At personal space personal space

5e. Touch
Describe (kind, frequency, duration):

5f. Silence
Describe (frequency, duration, intended and perceived meaning):

5g. Posture and body language
Describe:

5h. Dress and accessories
Describe:

DISCOVERABLE

6. Expectations of Communication Process

6a. Location of meaning

Explicit ———————————— Implied

6b. How meaning is created

Individual ———————————— Mutual

6c. Responsibility for understanding

Listener ———————————— Speaker

7. Nature of Topics Discussed

7a. Kinds of topics
___ personal, ___ familial, ___ professional, ___ political, ___ spiritual, ___ community, ___ other

7b. Level of self-disclosure

Open ———————————— Closed

8. Treatment of Emotion

8a. Openness to discuss feelings

Open ————|———— Reticent
      Subtle

8b. Method of expression

Expresses ———————————— Doesn't
openly   express

9. Permeability of New Ideas

Immediate ———————————— Extreme
openness   caution

10. Progress of Discussion

Expand/ ———————————— Contract/find
build   weaknesses

Note what you have learned about the different ways in which communication style behaviors are used and why:

[1] Note: In the book *Communication Highwire*, pages 123–171, extensive details are provided to give background on the development of this descriptor checklist, as well as over one hundred examples to give insight about the definition and application of the terms.

Communication Style Descriptor Checklist

FUNCTIONAL

11. Apologies

11a. Frequency

Constant |——|—— Intermittent —— Never

11b. Quantity

Many words ———————— Few words

11c. Timing

___ beginning, ___ middle, ___ end,
___ throughout, ___ in response to facts,
___ in response to emotions, ___ immediate,
___ after consideration, ___ never

11d. Purpose

___ admission of guilt/regret, ___ empathy,
___ social bonding, ___ courtesy, ___ other

11e. Content

General ———————— Specific

11f. Style

Describe:

12. Requests

12a. Frequency

Constant |——|—— Intermittent —— Never

12b. Quantity

Many words ———————— Few words

12c. Timing

___ beginning, ___ middle, ___ end,
___ throughout, ___ in response to facts,
___ in response to emotions, ___ immediate,
___ after consideration, ___ never

12d. Purpose

___ accomplish a task, ___ pay a compliment,
___ include someone, ___ assert authority,
___ encourage, ___ other

12e. Content

General ———————— Specific

12f. Style

Describe:

13. Praise

13a. Frequency

Constant |——|—— Intermittent —— Never

13b. Quantity

Many words ———————— Few words

13c. Timing

___ beginning, ___ middle, ___ end,
___ throughout, ___ in response to facts,
___ in response to emotions, ___ immediate,
___ after consideration, ___ never

13d. Purpose

___ relationship building, ___ request,
___ motivation, ___ confidence building,
___ criticism, ___ other

13e. Content

General ———————— Specific

13f. Style

Describe:

14. Disagreement

14a. Frequency

Constant |——|—— Intermittent —— Never

14b. Quantity

Many words ———————— Few words

14c. Timing

___ beginning, ___ middle, ___ end,
___ throughout, ___ in response to facts,
___ in response to emotions, ___ immediate,
___ after consideration, ___ never

14d. Purpose

___ improve process, ___ vent emotion,
___ learn, ___ courtesy,
___ disrupt forward movement, ___ other

14e. Content

General ———————— Specific

14f. Style

Describe:

15. Feedback

15a. Frequency

Constant |——|—— Intermittent —— Never

15b. Quantity

Many words ———————— Few words

15c. Timing

___ beginning, ___ middle, ___ end,
___ throughout, ___ in response to facts,
___ in response to emotions, ___ immediate,
___ after consideration, ___ never

15d. Purpose

___ correct, ___ encourage, ___ guide,
___ insult, ___ gain competitive edge,
___ assert power, ___ facilitate group-building,
___ other

15e. Content

___ specific , ___ general , ___ positive,
___ negative, ___ humorous, ___ other

15f. Style

Describe:

16. Humor and Joking

16a. Frequency

Constant |——|—— Intermittent —— Never

16b. Quantity

Many words ———————— Few words

16c. Timing

___ beginning, ___ middle, ___ end,
___ throughout, ___ in response to facts,
___ in response to emotions, ___ immediate,
___ after consideration, ___ never

16d. Purpose

___ lighten the mood/relieve tension,
___ empathize, ___ establish rapport,
___ criticize, ___ encourage, ___ other

16e. Content

Describe the topic (kind of info, topic, what it is poking fun at):

16f. Style

Describe:

Note what you have learned about different ways in which speech acts (apologies, requests, praise, disagreement, feedback, humor and joking) are used and why:

Source: Communication Highwire: Leveraging the Power of Diverse Communication Styles (Intercultural Press).
© 2005 Dianne Hofner Saphiere, Barbara Kappler Mikk, and Basma Ibrahim DeVries. All rights reserved.

Attachment C: Guidelines for Feedback Handout

1. What do you think or feel is positive about the communication style your colleague used in his or her e-mail? Describe a positive effect it could have on the receiver.

2. What you would change, if anything, about your colleague's communication style in this e-mail? Share possible negative effects the communication style might have and how you would suggest writing it instead.

Tips for International and Intercultural E-Mail

1. Use greetings and social expressions in the receiver's native language.
2. Use short sentences and vocabulary with clear meaning. Avoid idiomatic expressions. Use "standard" dictionary language.
3. Format your e-mail for easy review by a nonnative speaker. Use headings or section titles and numbers or bulleted points.
4. Consider adjusting your style to the receiver's style in order to motivate the receiver. Style switching can foster collaboration, while improving efficiency and task completion.

Reprinted with slight adaptation and permission from Dianne Hofner Saphiere, Barbara Kappler Mikk, and Basma Ibrahim DeVries, *Communication Highwire: Leveraging the Power of Diverse Communication Styles*, Intercultural Press, 2005, Activity 23, pages 242–247.

11

Toothpicks

Time Required:

45–60 minutes: 25–30 minutes for activity, 20–30 minutes to debrief

Objectives:

To help participants:

1. Explore how nonverbal communication impacts the message received.
2. Recognize the importance of learning the nonverbal rules of another culture.
3. Observe how nonverbal messages can be cultural and/or gender specific.
4. Experience silence as it impacts communication.
5. Experience the feeling of behaving inappropriately when the rules are unspoken.

Materials:

Flip chart or slide listing rules

Toothpicks (10 per participant)

Index cards with a "Nonverbal Rule" on each card

Eight different colored dots to code the cards that have the same nonverbal rule

Process:

1. Give each participant a card and explain the objectives of the activity.
2. Review these rules on the chart or slide:
   - Follow the rules on your card.
   - Talk with someone who has a different color dot on his or her card.
   - Do not share the "rule" on your card.
   - Try to figure out the difference in your nonverbal communication rules.

3. Ask participants to find someone with a card that has a different color dot from theirs and begin discussing a common topic (e.g., What is one of your favorite movies and why? Place to travel? Hobby or pastime?).
4. Tell participants that when the person they are speaking with violates their nonverbal rule, they are to give the person violating the rule a toothpick.
5. After 3–5 minutes, ask participants to switch to another person with yet a different color dot and repeat this several times.
6. After approximately 10 minutes call time and prepare to debrief.

Debriefing Questions:

1. What did it feel like to participate? To give toothpicks? To receive them?
2. How easy or hard was it to discover what someone else's nonverbal rules were?
3. What does this activity suggest about how easy or hard is it to interact when you don't know the rules?
4. Describe some nonverbal differences that you encountered. Are there other ways nonverbal behavior can differ?
5. How do nonverbal behaviors affect communication? Personal interactions? Perceptions of others?
6. Were you comfortable with periods of silence? How might that affect communication?

Debriefing Conclusions:

1. Nonverbal behavior can have a great impact on communication.
2. Learning the nonverbal "rules" in a new culture can help to prevent misunderstanding and personal embarrassment.
3. Many communication "rules" are taken for granted by the people within a culture. It is important to be observant and to ask appropriate cross-cultural questions to enhance understanding.
4. Silence may be a part of a communication style. Learning to allow for silence can enhance overall communication effectiveness.

Optional way to conduct the exercise:

You can add up toothpicks and the person with the fewest toothpicks wins a prize.

Nonverbal "Rules" for "Appropriate" Communication

(Print, cut, and paste on index cards or print directly on index cards)

1. You find direct eye contact offensive. When you speak, you try not to look people directly in the eye; instead, you avert your eye contact from listeners. If someone looks you in the eye, give him or her a toothpick.

2. You like to know that people are listening when you speak and you expect that people show they are listening by nodding their heads. You nod your head when others speak. When you are speaking, if listeners are not nodding their heads, give them each a toothpick.

3. You find people standing closer than 18 inches or half a meter away from you offensive. Stand at quite a distance from people and give them each a toothpick if they come too close.

4. During conversations you find tapping one's feet or fidgeting offensive. Try not to do this when you speak to people and give them each a toothpick if they do this when you are speaking with them.

5. You like when people get their ideas out quickly in conversations and you are easily distracted by vocalized fillers such as "um," "ah," and "er." If people do not speak quickly enough or if they use vocalized fillers, give them each a toothpick.

6. When speaking, you pause frequently and you do not like to be interrupted until you finish speaking. You do not interrupt others when they speak. If people interrupt you and do not give you enough time to pause, give them each a toothpick.

7. When listening carefully you stand with your arms folded firmly in front of you so that nothing can "intrude" on your attention. If your conversation partner is standing with a "relaxed" posture, give her or him a toothpick.

8. Smiling during a conversation indicates to you that the conversation is not being taken seriously. If your conversation partner is smiling while you talk, give him or her a toothpick.

This activity was adapted with permission from an activity created by Nicki Kukar and later modified by Jackie Spencer and Sylvie Bayart for Dianne Hofner Saphiere, Barbara Kappler Mikk, and Basma Ibrahim DeVries, *Communication Highwire: Leveraging the Power of Diverse Communication Styles*, Intercultural Press, 2005, Activity 24, pages 248–250.

Building Cultural Bridges to Communication

12

WORKPLACE
NONVERBAL
WRITTEN
M–H

Time Required:

90–120 minutes: 40–60 minutes for activity and 50–60 minutes to debrief

Objectives:

To help participants:

1. Identify barriers to cross-cultural communication.
2. Recognize cultural differences to the same barriers.
3. Discuss effect of barriers on relationships/productivity.
4. Develop strategies to decrease barriers.

Materials:

Cultural scenarios on index cards (1 for each group)

Intercultural Communication Handout for each participant

Process:

1. Introduce the objectives for this activity.
2. Distribute the Intercultural Communication Handout and briefly review.
3. Divide the group into teams of 4–6.
4. Have one member of each team draw a cultural scenario card.
5. Ask each team to read the scenario and identify barriers to communication.

Questions for Scenario Review:

- What communication barriers are evident in this scenario?
- What cultural factors may be related to the barrier(s)?
- How might the barrier(s) impact relationships? Team functioning? Workplace productivity?
- What specific behaviors could help decrease or remove the barrier(s)?

6. Have each team select one member to share the scenario and another team member to share the group thoughts/ suggestions.
7. Large group: Debrief with compare/contrast of cultural scenarios.

Debriefing Questions:

1. How did you feel during the team activity?
2. Which communication barriers were identified in these scenarios? Which barriers might be more salient? Less evident?
3. Have you observed or experienced something similar to one of these situations? Describe.
4. Which strategies would be most comfortable for you? More difficult? Why?
5. Did you have any insights into cross-cultural communication during your team activity? As you listened to the other scenarios?
6. How might this activity be helpful to you in the future?

Debriefing Conclusions:

1. Cultural preferences can impede effective cross-cultural communication.
2. Awareness of the cultural aspects of communication enhances understanding.
3. Many communication "rules" are taken for granted by the people within the culture.
4. Being observant and asking appropriate questions can enhance cross-cultural understanding.

Intercultural Communication Handout

Communication style preferences are learned and rooted within culture. We learn our culture from the "inside," so we tend to assume that everyone else views the world the same way we see the world. Even the mastery of a foreign language cannot guarantee an individual will meet with success in an intercultural setting. Awareness of these three aspects in cross-cultural communication can be used to enhance understanding:

External and Internal Culture

Whether a culture is national or organizational, it is important to be aware of the meaning that lies beneath observable behavior.

- External culture can be studied in history, geography, political science, and the arts. Understanding external, objective aspects of a culture can foster greater understanding.
- Internal culture is culture implicitly learned. Internal culture includes subjective knowledge that is unconsciously held, including shared values, beliefs, assumptions, and behaviors. Internal aspects of culture cause the greatest misunderstandings in cross-cultural encounters.

High Context and Low Context Cultures

Cultural communication falls along a continuum from high context cultures to low context cultures.

- High context cultures have a long tradition of commonly shared values and understandings. Communication is more implicit and internalized; it is transmitted in subtle ways. Nonverbal cues are very important. The environmental setting, gestures, and mood are part of the message being communicated.
- Low context cultures have a preference for explicit and direct information. Specific and in-depth explanations are the expected norm. In low context cultures, individuals are usually more competitive. They tend to be more analytic rather than holistic in their problem solving.

Monochronic and Polychronic Time

Differences in basic time systems are also a source of frustration and misunderstanding in cross-cultural communication. These are two different ways to perceive time. Each approach has advantages and disadvantages.

- Monochronic time usually is found in industrialized societies. Time is blocked into allotments and one task at a time takes precedence. When the scheduled time is "up" the person is expected to move on.
- Polychronic time means being involved with many different things at one time. There is no sense of "wasting time" or "running out of time." There is more of a focus on people and relationships. Time is experienced very differently.

Cultural Scenarios

You are German, working on a multicultural team in Belgium. You begin your work day at 08:00 and leave each day at 17:00. Several members of your team (from Spain and France) "wander in" well after 08:00, heading directly for coffee. These team members regularly arrive late and rarely offer a morning greeting. You do not respect their lack of punctuality and wonder how you will be able to work with them on the new assignment.

You are working as a purchasing agent for a boat repair company in the Seattle area. You are Taiwanese. You have been able to negotiate "best price" deals for your employer on parts from a Taiwan manufacturer. Today your U.S. employer has received some bad news and he is very angry about a family matter. He begins to yell at you, showing you no respect.

You are a thirty-year-old German female. Your company has recently purchased a Russian business and you are assigned to manage an office in a small Russian village. The current office supervisor is a fifty-five-year-old Russian male. He will remain in the office and report directly to you. All of the employees are Russian and they have been reporting directly to him.

You are a U.S. computer technology specialist working for a Chinese employer. You believe it is best to be very specific when working with a customer. Your employer takes a different approach. The company sales and service policy is not clear to you. You are wondering how you will define your area of responsibility.

You are a college student from Italy, enrolled in a U.S. university. Your roommate in the international dorm is from England. You like to invite classmates to visit you in your room. Your roommate does not approve of the visitors and does not seem interested in forming a friendship. You are wondering how you will last through the year.

You create a scenario that applies specifically to your organization.

Collaborative Connection, 2008 Sources: Sana Reynolds and Deborah Valentine, *Guide to Cross-Cultural Communication*, Pearson Education, 2004; Paul B. Pedersen, *110 Experiences for Multicultural Learning*, American Psychological Association, 2004; Patricia A. Cassiday, *Leadership in International Settings: Exploring the Values, Beliefs and Assumptions of Expatriates*, unpublished dissertation, 2004.

13

Are You Listening?

Time Required:

40–50 minutes: 5 minutes for instructions, 15 minutes for activity, 20–30 minutes to debrief

Objectives:

To help participants:

1. Recognize the difficulty in listening and retelling another person's story.
2. Identify why there may be a difference in what we hear and what was said.
3. Describe ways personal projections and interpretations of the listener can affect meaning/intention of the speaker.

Materials:

Cultural Clues Handout

Process:

1. Introduce the Cultural Clues Handout.
2. Ask participants to find a partner (someone they do not know very well).
3. Have one person speak first while the other person listens. The speaker uses the Cultural Clues Handout as a guide for a two-minute "cultural conversation."
4. Allow two minutes for the listener to repeat everything the speaker said, felt, and/or meant about his/her culture.
5. Provide the speaker and listener two minutes to discuss how accurately the listener was in understanding what was said.
6. Have the speaker and listener exchange roles and repeat the experience in new roles.

Debriefing Questions:

1. How did you define your "culture"? What aspects were most important to share? Did the listener identify the most important aspects from your message?
2. What was easiest for the listener to remember: specific facts, events, or feelings? Why?
3. How did you feel sharing your story? Repeating what you heard?
4. Were you surprised by any part of this exercise? Describe.
5. How might this exercise apply in a real-life setting?

Debriefing Conclusions:

1. Culture may be broadly defined to include ethnicity, nationality, gender, age, organizational affiliation, economic or social status.
2. Topics that are appropriate to share can differ considerably across cultures; when someone does/does not share what would be appropriate in our own culture, it can lead to misperceptions and mistrust.
3. What a person says and what we hear may differ based on our interpretation and/or cultural perspective.
4. It is often easier to remember specific information than to understand another person's feelings.
5. Listening, "hearing," and retelling a story require communication skills that can be consciously developed.

Cultural Clues Handout

Take a few minutes to review the bullets below. Each culture has preferences for what others "should know." Many cultures have topics that are not easily shared with others. Effectively dealing across cultures requires openness to difference.

Try to share something about your culture:

- Culture or ethnicity you identify with . . .
- "New information" for someone from another cultural background
- Behavior that could be "misinterpreted" by those outside of your culture
- A situation in which assumption of "sameness" might lead to misunderstanding
- An example of "family behavior" specific to your culture/ethnicity
- Something important for "others" to understand
- Nonverbal behaviors to watch for: important to respect
- Sayings, quotes, or proverbs that offer clues to "how we think"
- How important are words? Is it better to use fewer or more words?
- Cultural approach to being on time
- Symbols or signs of power/status
- Cultural preference toward "being on time"
- Approaches to "change": Feelings? Thoughts? Actions?
- "Insider" information
- In My Family . . .
- This behavior really "means this"
- Anything you believe is interesting and important to share

Collaborative Connection, 2008 Sources: Sharon A. Reyes, *Constructivist Strategies for Teaching English Language Learners*, Corwin Press, 2007; Paul B. Pedersen, *110 Experiences for Multicultural Learning*, American Psychological Association, 2004.

14

Communicating Policy in a Cultural Context

Time Required:

30–45 minutes: 10–15 minutes for activity, 20–30 minutes to debrief

Objectives:

To help participants:

1. Recognize the difficulty of interpreting policy statements in a multicultural setting.
2. Identify how culture influences word choice and omissions.
3. Describe ways cultural perspective may influence the interpretation of policy.

Materials:

One or more paragraphs from your organization's mission/vision statement or specific policy statement/regulation with 10–15 key words deleted. (Leave a blank space where words were deleted to allow for the participants to write in their own word choice.)

Copies of the original statement/policy.

Pencil or pen for each participant.

Process:

1. Give participants a copy of the statement with words deleted.
2. Ask participants to fill in words they consider appropriate for the missing spaces.
3. After approximately 10 minutes provide a copy of the original statement.
4. Compare the original with the various "alternative" wording.

Debriefing Questions:

1. How does your completed statement compare/contrast with the original?
2. What effect does your word choice have on the intent of the original policy?
3. What are similarities/differences in word choices among participants? Are there any culturally significant differences? Gender or age differences reflected in the choice of words/change in meaning?
4. Would any specific groups be advantaged/disadvantaged by the original policy statement?
5. What implications does this experience have for your organization? For cross-cultural effectiveness?

Debriefing Conclusions:

1. The mission/vision or written policies of the organization may have unintended cultural implications.
2. Cultural perspective can influence the interpretation of organizational policy.
3. Simple changes in word choice can make significant changes in meaning.
4. Some groups may be advantaged or disadvantaged by organizational policies—often unintentionally—unless they are reviewed with a cross-cultural lens.

Optional ways to conduct the exercise:

1. In an educational setting, this exercise can be used with faculty/administrators to identify how their policies (individual classroom policies or educational institution policies) might affect different student populations.
2. In an educational setting, this exercise can be used with students to increase their cross-cultural awareness by examining how the educational institution's policies and services might differentially impact different student groups.

Adapted from an activity by Paul Pedersen in W. H. Weeks, P. B. Pedersen, and R. W. Brislin. (1977). *A Manual of Structured Experiences for Cross-Cultural Learning.* Yarmouth, ME: Intercultural Press.

15

Can Anyone Hear Me?

Time Required:

50–60 minutes: 30 minutes for activity, 20–30 minutes for debrief

Objectives:

To help participants:

1. Identify how culture preferences such as assertiveness, persuasive argument, and preference for debate can affect team atmosphere and productivity.
2. Gain awareness of cultural impact on group interaction.
3. Gain insight into how a discussion may be impacted by the dominance of a few members.

Materials:

One sentence that summarizes a current issue with which the group is struggling. For example:

- Should we allow people to attend staff meetings virtually?
- Should the person who wrote a report make the presentation to the executive team, even if she or he is not the most senior member of the team?
- Who should represent the team at the conference in Hawaii— and why?
- Should teams be allowed to develop a single report that represents collective work or should individuals be required to do their own reports to demonstrate their knowledge/competence?

Process:

1. Divide participants into groups of 10–15.
2. Have groups form a communication circle for a "turn-taking" activity.
3. Give each member the opportunity to make one statement or express one idea, related to the topic. (Only one idea may be expressed during each turn.)

4. Let each person in the circle have an opportunity to make one uninterrupted statement.
5. Continue this turn-taking process around the circle as many times as necessary until every member has expressed everything she/he wishes to contribute.
6. Allow members who have nothing more to contribute to simply say "I pass" until no one in the circle has anything left to contribute.

Debriefing Questions:

1. How is this communication process different from the process usually used to discuss issues on this team?
2. How did this process feel to you? How does your personal preference for discussion affect the way you felt during this process?
3. What effect do you think this process had on the outcome of the discussion?
4. How could cultural preferences affect responses to this process?
5. How might insight from this activity help you improve discussions in the future?

Debriefing Conclusions:

1. Individuals who prefer a more expressive form of communication may feel uncomfortable with a "turn taking" process.
2. Individuals who have a more reflective communication style may find this process more comfortable.
3. Establishing "turn taking" guidelines can:
   a. help to balance unequal power distribution
   b. enhance opportunities to hear the perspectives of quieter members who may not otherwise contribute
   c. increase group productivity/creativity by expanding choices/options
4. Alternating a "turn taking" process with a more "free flowing" process can create a team environment that allows both expressive and reflective communicators to feel valued.

   Note: This exercise is particularly useful for intact work teams experiencing challenges related to some members being particularly quiet during group meetings while others dominate conversations.

Collaborative Connection, 2008 Sources: Sana Reynolds and Deborah Valentine, *Guide to Cross-Cultural Communication*, Pearson Education, 2004; Paul B. Pedersen, *110 Experiences for Multicultural Learning*, American Psychological Association, 2004; Craig Storti, *Cross-Cultural Dialogues: 74 Brief Encounters with Cultural Difference*, Intercultural Press, 1994.

16

Communication Solutions

Time Required:

100–120 minutes: 10 minute introduction, Six 10 minute rounds, 30 minutes to debrief

Objectives:

Help participants learn to:

1. Identify a variety of communication challenges.
2. Generate multiple options for resolving each problem.
3. Create an opportunity to improve the solutions.
4. Explore a wide range of perspectives/roles when approaching the problem.

Materials:

Sample Communication Problem Handout for each individual

Work Sheets—one for each team

Organization specific issues or 4 × 6 index cards with communication challenges

Pens or pencils

Process:

1. Ask participants to count off from 1 to 6 (creating 6 equal teams).
2. Distribute the Sample Communication Problem Handout to each participant and one Work Sheet to each team.
3. Describe the process and timeframe, giving participants the "big picture." This activity consists of six rounds (approximately 10 minutes each).
4. Review the Sample Communication Problem handout.

Give the instructions in steps 5–10

5. **Round 1:** Each team identifies (or draws) a workplace communication problem. Discussion of the problem includes:
   1) identifying the context in which the problem occurs;
   2) identifying the employees involved with the problem;
   3) recognizing who "owns" the problem; then 4) exploring the gap between the desired goal and current situation.

6. **Round 2:** Each team passes its problem to the team on its left. The second team serves as the consultant team. You have approximately 10 minutes to review the problem and write some possible solutions. Use the handout as a sample.

7. **Round 3:** Pass the problem and solutions on to the next team. In the third round, you are now "cynical critics." Read the problem and possible solutions. Your goal is to identify any weaknesses, limitations, or negative consequences for the solution section. Only emphasize the negative; ignore all positive aspects of the solution. (See the critique section of the handout.)

8. **Round 4:** Pass the worksheet (problem, solution, and critique) to the next team. In round 4 the team reviews the problem and solution. The goal is to identify strengths, virtues, and positive consequences for the solution. Write a short assessment of the solution that ignores all negative aspects.

9. **Round 5:** Pass the packet (problem, solution, critique, positive assessment) to the next team. Review the problem, solution, critique, and positive assessment, then suggest an improved solution to the original problem. Refer to Improved Solution on the handout.

10. **Round 6:** Pass all material to the team that originated the problem. Allow time for team to review the solutions and discuss. The team should evaluate the suggestions and solutions; discussing the relative effectiveness of each.

11. Debrief in large groups. Teams report on their communication problem and the "best" solution.

Debriefing Questions:

1. How did you feel about the process for generating and/or enhancing solutions to communication problems? Alternate applications?

2. Describe any new insights you have about the process or discussion, which were most useful in handling communication problems.

3. Which of the roles was most comfortable? Least comfortable? Why? Review each of the roles: Owner of the problem; Consultant; Critic; Booster; Enhancer; and Evaluator

4. Did your own communication style preferences impact your participation in any of the various "roles"? Your cultural preferences? Gender?

5. How might you use this process—or something similar—in your real life?

Debriefing Conclusions:

1. Communication problems are common in multicultural groups and between departments with different objectives/ perspectives.

2. Identified communication problems can be resolved by a variety of methods.

3. Applying multiple perspectives to a problem can generate a variety of suggestions and thus enhance the effectiveness of the solutions.

4. Cultural issues can affect comfort level with different roles. For example, someone who is comfortable with direct, confrontational communication may feel more comfortable being a "critic" than someone who has learned culturally that disagreement—especially direct and/or with someone who has authority—is inappropriate.

5. Communication solutions are most effective when they match the preferred style of the individual or group or when presented with style preference in mind.

Adapted from a framework by Sivasailam Thiagarajan.

Sample Communication Problems

1. A large organization has training/staff development departments located in three centralized areas, worldwide. Currently, each of these hubs is operating independently with different approaches and expectations for training objectives and outcomes. These three staff development hubs are composed of specialists with expertise in specific disciplines. The new organizational leaders wish to implement a unified approach to staff development across the three diverse hubs. The communication challenge is delivering a uniformly consistent message as to "how things are done here", emphasizing the importance and value of consistency while enhancing the quality of the product.

2. Several Asian employees in the accounting department have requested transfers from the accounting department to other assignments. Upon investigation, you find one of the team leaders in accounting, Margaret, supervises all of the Asian employees requesting transfers. Margaret recently was promoted to team leader based on exceptional ratings in her job performance as an accountant. It appears that Margaret's communication style, as a new team leader, may be adversely affecting performance in the accounting department.

3. You are the president of a technology company that has recently merged with a new start-up organization. Since the acquisition of this new company, you are finding performance teams are struggling to produce results. The generational composition of your original employee group was mainly 30- to 40-year-olds, with 10+ years of experience. The new employees are generally in their 20s and recent college graduates, who are new to the field. Facilitating productive communication and teamwork is a serious challenge within the new organizational structure.

4. You are the head of the customer service at the community bank. One of your bank managers, George, has been the focus of several complaints from the female employees in his department. The complaints include disrespect, condescension, inappropriate comments of a sexual nature, and discomfort with proximity. The male employees under George's supervision have not filed any complaints. It appears that George has difficulty communicating with his female employees. When you approach George with this problem, he appears surprised and confused by the female complaints.

5. Lorraine is one of your top managers. She is bright, hard-working, and conscientious. Lorraine expresses a commitment to collaboration, teaming, and facilitation of group problem solving. During your observations of several team sessions, Lorraine has become impassioned, taking over the group discussion and driving home her perspective. It appears difficult for her to facilitate discussions that generate multiple perspectives. Her style, which is perceived as argumentative, tends to limit discussion and hamper the potential for creativity. Lorraine is open to discussing the impact of her style but seems unclear on how to improve her communication.

Sample Communication Problem Handout

Problem

Your organization is going through restructuring and change. You need input from all departments to ensure the success of the overall transformation. In an attempt to be proactive, you have asked Jim to pull together division heads from sales, marketing, engineering, finance, and production. The communication objective is to encourage the participants' commitment and contribution to the upcoming change process. At the end of Jim's 45-minute presentation, he opens the meeting for discussion. The room is silent.

1. Context: Corporate Headquarters
2. Employees involved: Corporate leaders, division chiefs, Jim
3. "Owner" of the problem: Jim, corporate leaders
4. Objective: promote communication
5. Status: communication shut-down

Solution

1. Use a set of "initial" topics to start off the discussion.
2. Separate the participants into smaller groups by department. Allow time to process the information in the smaller group.

Critique

1. Unfortunately, Jim's presentation may have been well thought out and strategic from his point of view, yet missed the objective completely for his range of participants. The first solution assumes Jim has presented the information in such a way that his diverse audience is now focusing in on the common good of the organization. The silence indicates that Jim failed to establish common ground and commitment. Introducing specific topics related to change, resiliency, productivity, and so on at this point may be counterproductive.
2. The second solution may also defeat the purpose of the presentation. Separating the larger group into smaller groups may promote departmental self-interest and/or individual self-interest, entrenching participants farther into their departmental rather than organizational perspectives. Jim will have little control over the direction the small group discussions take, resulting in less, rather than more, organizational coherence.

Positive Assessment

1. There is no one right way to communicate the need for change to all employees. Assuming that Jim has taken difference in communication style into consideration when designing his presentation, he can now use a variety of questions to stimulate the group discussion. How do you *see* this change? What did you *hear* in the presentation? How do you *feel* about our next steps? Do you have some data that supports your position? Can we generate several choices?
2. The second solution also has merit. Coming together in the smaller groups may help those with similar style and background focus on the concepts and discuss the information. The

small groups can respond to specifics for the change from their area of expertise and then contribute to whole group solution through the group voice. Individuals might be hesitant to speak up alone whereas speaking as a group may help them be more candid.

Improved Solution

It can be helpful to send some information out to participants prior to the presentation, especially when dealing with restructuring and change. Prior knowledge allows for individuals to assimilate the information and prepare for discussion.

Jim is addressing a very diverse audience. It is important that he considered the style preferences of the participants in the design of the presentation. The topic is likely charged with emotion, so building intermittent discussion topics within the course of the presentation may encourage greater participation, while stimulating additional thought and broadening the insights.

Jim may wish to follow up the whole group discussion with a second meeting the following week, allowing time for department leaders to reflect on and process the information. Communication is enhanced when there is a sense of respect and trust among participants. A second meeting should reflect the contributions of the group during the first session (across departmental interests). The organization will benefit from additional time spent on developing collaborative communication.

Adapted from a framewok by Sivasailam Thiagarajan.

Work Sheet: Team Name _____

THE PROBLEM:

THE SOLUTION:

CRITIQUE:

POSITIVE ASSESSMENT:

IMPROVED SOLUTION:

17

Persuasion

Time Required:

30–60 minutes

Objectives:

To help participants:

1. Identify several persuasive communication styles.
2. Explore critical factors associated with effective communication.
3. Experience a safe role-play opportunity for persuasive communication.
4. Generate a variety of ways to enhance communication.
5. Explore concepts of organizational change.

Materials:

> Handout on Persuasive Communication (Attachment A)
>
> Pre- and Post-test questionnaire for each participant (Attachment B)
>
> Role Assignments—four versions on different-colored paper or cards (Attachment C)
>
> Timer and whistle

Process:

1. Read and discuss persuasive communication (Attachment A).
2. Ask participants to complete pretest questionnaire (Attachment B).
3. Collect completed questionnaires.
4. Have each participant draw a "role" assignment (Attachment C) and read their "role." Stress the importance of sticking as close as possible to their role.
5. Ask participants to move to a corner of the room labeled for the role groups. "Structural change" should be diagonally

across from "training position." "Deterministic approach" should be diagonal from "opportunistic approach." (Each group should have 5–10 members.)

6. Strategy Development in groups (7 minutes):
Ask participants to discuss roles and develop strategies to persuade others.
Suggestions:
   - Develop a clear and compelling message to deliver.
   - Create a logical argument to support your position.
   - Share personal anecdotes to support your position.

7. Conversation Period (10 minutes):
Ask participants to have one-on-one conversations with the individuals in the groups to their right or left. The communication goal is to engage in conversations rather than try to "deliver a message."

8. Post Test: Redistribute the questionnaire and ask the participants to complete it once again. Quickly count the results and tally choices (Attachment B).

Debriefing:

1. Share the pretest scores between structural change and training.
2. Do participants predict a change in the post test? Why? Why not?
3. Announce results. Discuss differences or lack of differences.
4. Share the pretest scores between deterministic/opportunistic approaches.
5. Do participants predict a change in the post test? Why? Why not?
6. Announce results. Discuss differences or lack of differences.

Debriefing Questions:

1. Was your strategy the original strategy developed by the group or did you change it? If so, why?
2. Was your pretest choice different from the position assigned to you? How did the difference impact your persuasion strategy?
3. What type of strategies did others use to persuade you? Which strategies were most effective? Ineffective?
4. Did you have a real conversation with other people you met? Did you actively listen to their message?
5. Did you change your position between the pre- and post-test? If yes, what persuaded you?

Debriefing Conclusions:

1. Persuasive communication styles may be more effective or less effective based on the preference of the receiver.
2. Several factors should be considered when developing a persuasive strategy.
3. Enhanced communication can lead to organizational innovation.
4. Role playing can assist in the development of effective persuasive strategies.

Adapted from an activity by Sivasailam Thiagarajan, *Thiagi's 100 Favorite Games*, John Wiley and Sons, Inc., 2006.

Attachment A: Persuasive Communication

We have all been in a position where we need to convince someone about something. We use persuasion to influence the other person toward an idea, an attitude, or an action. Persuasive communication tries to convince the listener toward a particular side of a debatable position. We may choose from a variety of techniques when trying to influence the listener. Persuasive communication is most effective when the message appeals to the "style" of the receiver. Some persuasive approaches include:

- *Credibility:* Make your position believable by developing clarity in communication: use clear and concise language, eliminate contradictory information.
- *Rational Appeal:* Build consensus by engaging the listener's rationality; take a logical approach; use tangible evidence to make your position credible.
- *Logic:* Use specific data, logical arguments, details, or proof that can be measured to support your position.
- *Authority:* Offer quotes, statements, research from authorities in the field; specifics from personal experience can enhance your persuasiveness.
- *Emotional Appeal:* Build empathy with the listener by appealing to feelings/emotions; communicate with enthusiasm, excitement, and/or passion about the topic.
- *Originality:* Express your position in a new, creative, or novel way; engage the listener from an original perspective.

Communication is most convincing when built upon shared interests of the individuals or the organization. With the focus on recipient style, choose persuasive language, words that actively engage the listener in considering your position. Anticipate opposing arguments and be prepared to clarify the issue from your position. Clarity in explaining the key issues will add to the persuasiveness of your argument. Developing a set of flexible, influential strategies can greatly enhance your power of persuasion.

Adapted from an activity by Sivasailam Thiagarajan, *Thiagi's 100 Favorite Games*, John Wiley and Sons, Inc., 2006.

Attachment B: Pre- and Post-Test Questionnaire: Organizational Culture Change

Topic I: Which of these is the more effective way to make your organization more innovative?

_____ Position 1: Make *structural changes* altering the reporting relationships in the organizational chart and modify the way employees solve problems and resolve conflicts.

_____ Position 2: *Provide training* designed to help employees master new skills, knowledge, and attitudes related to organizational innovation.

Topic II: Which of these is the most effective way to implement our design for increased organizational innovation?

_____ Position 1: Take a *deterministic approach*. Have a specific plan and stick to it.

_____ Position 2 Take an *opportunistic approach*. Be flexible and depart from the plan whenever appropriate.

Adapted from an activity by Sivasailam Thiagarajan, *Thiagi's 100 Favorite Games*, John Wiley and Sons, Inc., 2006.

Attachment C

Role Assignment 1

Make structural changes. Altering reporting relationships in the organizational chart and modifying the ways employees solve problems and resolve conflicts.

- Play the role of a person who believes structural change is the most effective way to make our organization more innovative. (Set aside your personal position if it is different from this position.)
- During the conversation period, your mission is to persuade others to accept this position.

Role Assignment 2

Provide training. Help employees master new skills, knowledge, and attitudes related to organizational innovation.

- Play the role of a person who believes that training is the most effective way to make our organization more innovative. (Set aside your personal position if it is different from this position.)
- During the conversation period, your mission is to persuade others to accept this position.

Role Assignment 3

Take a deterministic approach. Have a specific plan and stick to it.

- Play the role of a person who holds this deterministic position when trying to make our organization more innovative. (Set aside your personal position if it is different from this position.)
- During the conversation period, your mission is to persuade others to accept this position.

Role Assignment 4

Take an opportunistic approach. Be flexible and depart from the plan whenever appropriate.

- Play the role of a person who holds this opportunistic position when trying to make our organization more innovative. (Set aside your personal position if it is different from this position.)
- During the conversation period, your mission is to persuade others to accept this position.

Adapted from an activity by Sivasailam Thiagarajan, *Thiagi's 100 Favorite Games*, John Wiley and Sons, Inc., 2006.

18

My Rule/Your Rule

Time Required:

60 minutes: 15 minutes to set up, 20 minutes in groups, 25 minutes to report back and debrief

Objectives:

To help participants:

1. Experience identifying another person's perspective and explaining that perspective in neutral, nonjudgmental language.
2. Identify ways of asking for clarification about another person's behavior.

WORKPLACE
EDUCATION
VERBAL
NONVERBAL
M–H

Materials:

Miniature case studies or quotes relevant to your audience (sample quotes appear on page 79)

Flip chart paper

Markers

Process:

1. Have quotes or miniature cases in large print posted around the room. One quote or case per sheet of paper.
2. Demonstrate the process you want the participants to engage in. Have one piece of flip chart paper taped horizontally on the wall. Draw a line down the middle and a line across the top.

52 ACTIVITIES FOR IMPROVING CROSS-CULTURAL COMMUNICATION   **77**

Use an example, such as "Why didn't she just tell me she didn't understand?"

Ask the group, "Who are the actors in this situation?" Write these two words on either side of the middle line.

Next, ask "What are the perspectives of these two people on this situation?"

For example: The professor wants to teach as efficiently as possible and needs each student to tell him when they don't understand. The professor wants to be sure each student learns as much as possible. The student values hierarchy and does not want to embarrass the professor or have the professor lose face by telling him that his instructions were not clear.

Elicit from the group the potential perspectives from each person's point of view. If you get negative or judgmental responses, ask the group to reframe the behavior in neutral or positive language from the perspective of the person exhibiting the behavior.

Now ask the group to identify how the person asking the question could approach the other person to get clarification on what is really motivating their behavior—with attention to the other person's preferred communication style.

For example, the professor might approach the student and say

- If the student's communication style is direct: "I see that you didn't understand the original instructions. Can you tell me what would have helped you ask me for clarification?"
- If the student's communication style is indirect: "I am curious about how people seek clarification. Tell me about a time when someone you know received unclear instructions and how they might have gotten more clarification."

3. Ask participants to walk around the room and choose a quote that is most interesting to them. Ensure there are at least three people at each quote. Ask them to take a flip chart and markers as a group and complete these steps:
   - Identify the two people involved in this situation. Write their title/roles at the top of the page.
   - Identify the multiple perspectives for each person that might be informing their thinking and record those reasons under their title.
   - Be sure the perspectives are framed neutrally and nonjudgmentally.
   - Develop at least two ways that the person quoted can ask the other person what their behavior really means. Each question should assume a different communication style on the part of the person being questioned. Identify the communication style of that person based on the question.

4. After 20 minutes, ask each group to report to the larger group, identifying the quote; the two people; *one* of the perspectives they identified for each person; and the question they identified for seeking clarification. (Note: The question is the most important thing to report here because it is the communication they are going to use to begin clarification. If you have little time, ask them to report the question only.)
5. Debrief the experience.

Debriefing Questions:

1. What part of this exercise was hardest to do? Easiest? Why?
2. How can you apply this experience to your everyday life?

Debriefing Conclusions:

1. Perspective taking and frame shifting are critical skills for effective intercultural communication.
2. Building empathy, or the ability to try to see from the perspective of another person, is central to facilitating understanding in perplexing situations. The challenge in developing these skills is to engage ambiguity, suspend certainty, and think broadly and creatively outside one's usual frame of reference to uncover what might be underlying another person's perspective.
3. Once we have expanded our perspective and generated as many possible explanations for a behavior as possible, it is still important to check our reality with the other person.
4. Checking reality with another person requires that we generate a question that matches the other person's preferred communication style.

Caution for trainers:

This is an advanced exercise so it is not uncommon to hear language that is biased, negative, and/or judgmental. The facilitator should correct judgmental language by asking the entire group how else they might state any judgmental language that occurs.

Sample Quotes:

- Why is my academic advisor not advising me?
- Why do we spend so much time doing group work and talking instead of the professor teaching us?
- Why didn't she just tell me she did not understand the instructions?
- Why don't the Asian students participate in class?
- Why did my professor say she didn't know the answer to that question?

- Why doesn't the immigrant employee participate in staff meetings?
- Why doesn't my male manager give me feedback like he gives my male colleagues?
- Why doesn't my colleague ever look at me when he is talking to me?
- Why does my male colleague always stand so close and touch me when he is talking to me?

Adapted from an activity by Karen Rolston, Associate Director, UBC Centre for Intercultural Communication, *karen.rolston@ubc.ca*. Thank you to Sally McLean for developing a variation of this activity as the last stage (application stage) in a BARNGA debrief.

19

Thought Bubble Role-Plays

Time Required:

60 minutes: 5 minutes to set up, 20 minutes in small groups, 20–25 minutes (5 minutes per group) to demonstrate role-play and for large group to discuss strategies to bridge the gap, 10 minutes final debrief

Objectives:

To help participants:

1. Uncover possible perspectives underlying a misunderstanding.
2. Explore different and equally valid ways of looking at the same situation.
3. Practice paradigm shifting to "see" and "hear" different perspectives through the thought bubbles.

Materials:

Case studies (see samples on page 85)

Flip chart

Markers

Process:

1. Set up the activity with an example, such as this one below. First, read the dialogue only.

   A: Welcome to Canada, Alain. I'm looking forward to being your graduate supervisor.

   B: I'm very excited to be here, Dr. Johnston.

   A: I thought we'd start with looking at some of the recent findings in your specific area of interest. Take a look through this peer review journal and come back to me on Monday with your critiques.

   B: Yes, Dr. Johnston.

On Monday

A: So, how did it go? Let's look at some of your critiques.

B: I didn't actually do any critiques—I wanted to discuss the articles with you and hear your opinion first.

A: Really?!

2. Read the dialogue again—and this time insert the thought bubbles in italics. (It can be effective to have a co-facilitator or one of the participants read the thought bubbles and another person read the narrative.)

Oh good. Here is my new graduate student. He certainly comes highly recommended.

A: Welcome to Canada, Alain. I'm looking forward to being your graduate supervisor.

B: I'm very excited to be here, Dr. Johnston.

I'm so pleased to have been accepted to work with Dr Johnston. She's the best in our field.

A: I thought we'd start by looking at some of the recent findings in your specific area of interest. Look through this peer review journal and come back to me on Monday with your critiques.

These articles are a great way to dive right in and find out what his thinking is on this new research.

B: Yes, Dr. Johnston.

Ah . . . okay . . . I'm not sure what she's asking me to do. Who am I, a brand new graduate student, to be critiquing these research articles. They were written by tenured professors and have already been peer reviewed. What could I possibly say to critique them? I don't understand.

On Monday.

A: So, how did it go? Let's look at some of your critiques.

I'm looking forward to hearing his thoughts. This should be interesting.

B: I didn't actually do any critiques—I wanted to discuss the articles with you and hear your opinion first.

The articles were excellent and clearly well researched. I hope I will be able to contribute to the field as these researchers have. I don't want to overstep my status as a graduate student, however, and feel I should ask her opinion before giving my own.

A: Really?!

Oh no! I thought this fellow was supposed to be one of the best and brightest in our department!? Did he not understand my instructions? Or perhaps he was too busy getting settled into his new apartment to really think about studying, which would not be a good sign.

3. Have participants brainstorm the potential reasons, including both personal and cultural differences, that might have lead to this misunderstanding.
   - Person A values equality and is treating Person B as a colleague; Person B values hierarchy/status and does not feel it is appropriate to express an opinion before Person A does so.
   - Person A believes in getting right down to business and wants to start Person B on his academic journey immediately; Person B values relationship and doesn't feel comfortable expressing an academic opinion before he has a relationship and some understanding of Person A.
   - Person B is insecure and needs to be told how valuable his opinion is and encouraged to see himself as capable.

4. Have the group quickly create a new dialogue that has Person A and Person B getting to know each other a bit, has Person A explaining how pleased she is to have Person B as a colleague, telling Person B how she likes to work and asking Person B to describe his preferred work style.

5. Explain that they will be building Thought Bubble Dialogues like this in small groups.

6. Divide the participants into groups of four. Give each group one short incident with an intercultural miscommunication (see samples on page 85).

7. Give groups 15–20 minutes to read their scenario and prepare a role-play to present to the entire group, including:
   - Create a dialogue of approximately 4–5 exchanges between the individuals, including the thought bubbles that the two people might be thinking during the dialogue. (Remind the groups to suspend judgment, be curious, and seek to uncover both perspectives in a neutral way.)
   - Identify the potential reasons for the misunderstanding.
   - Return to the dialogue, creating a new communication that might help avoid the initial misunderstanding.

8. Ask groups to report back to present their interaction, including the thought bubbles; share the sources of miscommunica-

tion they have identified; and deliver a second dialogue that might avoid, or reduce, the miscommunication that occurred in the first dialogue.

9. After each role-play, leave time for comments from the large group on the possible root of the misunderstanding or miscommunication and possible strategies for bridging the communication gap. Collect the strategies on flip chart paper for the group to have at the end of the debrief.

Debriefing Questions:

1. What was most challenging about this exercise?
2. How can you use this experience in your day-to-day life?

Optional way to conduct the exercise:

This activity works well with a group of 16–20 participants. With more than 5 small groups or if time is short, it is possible to give the same scenarios to multiple groups and have them role-play for each other rather than for the entire group.

Adapted from an activity by Karen Rolston, Associate Director, UBC Centre for Intercultural Communication, *karen.rolston@ubc.ca*. Thank you to Mackie Chase for her inspiration on initially conceptualizing this activity.

Sample Scenarios

1. A new employee is told that success requires being a good team player. She believes that means agreeing with group consensus. The team leader believes it means challenging one another's ideas to create the greatest innovation.
2. A family moves into a new country. The wife/mother believes neighbors should welcome newcomers and waits to be greeted. Her neighbor believes newcomers should introduce themselves first. These two women meet in the local meat market.
3. A new employee does not understand the many acronyms used in the opening meeting his first day at work. The manager believes that if someone doesn't understand it is important that they ask.
4. A new employee is working in a language that is not her first language. She is struggling to learn her second language but is consistently interrupted by a coworker who, with the best of intentions, finishes her sentences for her.
5. A new manager enters the workplace to introduce himself. Immediately his assistant, a young, energetic female, introduces herself. During the introduction, she touches him and stands very close. He believes her physical contact is inappropriate.

Adapted from an activity by Karen Rolston, Associate Director, UBC Centre for Intercultural Communication, *karen.rolston@ubc.ca*. Thank you to Mackie Chase for her inspiration on initially conceptualizing this activity.

20

Different Days—Different Ways

Time Required:

60 Minutes: 5 minutes to set up, 15 minutes to complete Assessment Form, 20 minutes in small group, 20 minutes to debrief

Objectives:

To help participants:

1. Gain a more accurate assessment of the similarities and differences people will face after entering a new cultural context.
2. Consider the mental and behavioral alterations it might be necessary for individuals to make as they seek to adjust to their new realities.
3. Have conversations with others in new cultural surroundings, to assess the accuracy of personal assessments.

Materials:

One Assessment Form for each participant

Process:

1. Distribute the Assessment Form, and explain the task.
   a. Ask participants to identify those things they appreciated about their "old" culture. For example, how people greet each other at the beginning of the day; how meetings or classes are conducted (formally vs. informally); how work is assigned (with detail vs. generalities); how meals are experienced (individually or in group); forms of recreation; definitions of a "good" member of the culture; daily routines; personal hygiene and dress; and so on.
   b. Ask them to then identify those things they appreciate about their "new" culture.
   c. Point out that the more specific they can be in their descriptions, the more they are likely to benefit from the exercise.

2. Place participants in small groups of 3–4 to share their Assessment Forms and discuss the questions at the end of the form.
3. Bring the group back together for debriefing.

Debriefing Questions:

1. How did you feel when you were completing the Assessment Form?
2. How easy was it for you to identify cultural behaviors you appreciate in the "old" and "new" cultures? Why?
3. What observations did you make in your discussion? What did you notice?
4. What communication strategies did you identify that could help you explore cultural behaviors in your "new" culture?
5. What implications do these insights have for your adjustment to the "new" culture?

Debriefing Conclusions:

1. Each culture (national, regional, workplace) has its own way of doing things—what we consider "normal" in one culture can be seen as inappropriate, or less effective, in another.
2. Identifying those things we have become accustomed to—and like—in our "old" culture and those we struggle with in our "new" culture can help us understand the places in which we may be experiencing discomfort.
3. Sharing our reactions to both the "old" and the "new" with others can help us identify where adapting to the "new" culture can be useful. It can also help us find places where we might contribute to the "new" culture by sharing something from our "old" culture.
4. Considering effective communication strategies for discussing these insights can help us avoid unintended consequences of talking in a manner that might feel like a criticism of our "new" culture.

Ways to use the exercise:

This exercise can be useful for people facing significant transitions including a job change from one company to another, or a move to another state or region of their own home country.

This exercise can also be used at various stages of an international sojourn/study abroad cycle including predeparture, initial entry into the host culture, prereentry before coming home, and during the reentry process. It can also be applied for in-bound and outbound international students, international high school exchange program participants, individuals preparing for international business assignments, service-learning internship candidates, and families, corporate personnel, global nomads, and others dealing with readjustment after the return home.

Adapted from an exercise designed by Dr. Bruce La Brack, School of International Studies, University of the Pacific. This exercise was originally developed to assist outbound study abroad students to anticipate the impact of entering another culture in terms of the differences they were likely to encounter between their "typical home schedule" and "a typical day abroad."

Assessment Form

Behaviors I appreciate about my "old" culture	The purpose these behaviors served for the culture

Behaviors I find challenging in my "new" culture	The purpose these behaviors serve for the culture

Small group discussion questions: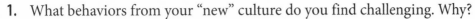

1. What behaviors from your "new" culture do you find challenging. Why?
2. What questions could you ask of someone in the "new" culture to better understand the history and purpose for the behaviors you have noticed?
3. What behaviors from your "old" culture do you believe would benefit your "new" culture? Why?
4. What questions could you ask of someone in the "new" culture that might help you understand if they would be open to different ways of doing things?
5. Who could you have this discussion with? What communication style and/or tools could you use to make this conversation most effective?

Adapted from an exercise designed by Dr. Bruce La Brack, School of International Studies, University of the Pacific. This exercise was originally developed to assist outbound study abroad students to anticipate the impact of entering another culture in terms of the differences they were likely to encounter between their "typical home schedule" and "a typical day abroad."

21

Building Team Communication

Time Required:

90 minutes: 20 minutes to review styles, 10 minutes to place profiles on chart, 30 minutes to discuss team implications, 30 minutes to decide how the team will communicate

Objective:

To help teams understand a range of communication styles, to identify each member's individual preferences, and to identify how they can create a team communication profile while honoring individual preferences.

Materials:

Style Profile Sheet with Descriptions (Attachment A)

One Style Profile Sheet for each participant (Attachment B)

One Style Profile Sheet—Attachment B blown up to 18″ × 24″ size—for each table of 4–6 participants.

Colored pens—one color for each team member

Process:

1. Describe each communication style, providing each team member with a copy of the Style Profile Sheet and the style definitions. Take time after describing each continuum to get participants to identify how people with different styles on each continuum might perceive and/or label those with other styles on that same continuum.
2. Ask each team member to use the Style Profile Sheet to create their own personal profile by placing an X on each line where their *preferred style* lies. Draw a line connecting the Xs, thereby plotting the individual style profile.
3. Using the Team Profile Sheet, ask each member to place their style profile on the sheet using a different color for each team member.

4. Use the completed Team Profile Sheet to discuss implications for the profile in creating advantages/challenges for the team. Watch for:
    a. Styles that are missing from the team—could this create challenges in communicating with a client who uses a style they don't have on their team?
    b. Styles in which the team is split—what could be the misperceptions that could occur? How can they avoid those misperceptions?
    c. Styles in which an individual or a small percentage of the team is different from the team, which could create unintentional isolation or negative impressions and treatment of the outliers.
5. Use the completed Team Profile Sheet and the discussion about implications to identify specific group norms for managing style differences. For example,
    a. If there is a time crunch, direct communication will be expected and accepted; if there is not, indirectness will be accepted without negative judgment.
    b. Attached communication will be accepted without negative judgment, AND a detached communicator can ask that the conversation take a less passionate tone on occasion.

Debriefing Questions:

1. What did you learn about your team during this process?
2. How will this process benefit your team? You personally?

Debriefing Conclusions:

1. Understanding the preferred styles of individual team members can allow members to avoid misperceptions and conflict based on style differences.
2. A team can create norms that expect certain styles to be used at certain times but that also allow each member to use their preferred style under some circumstances so that no individual is being asked to adapt 100 percent of the time.
3. Team members are willing to adapt their styles when necessary and still feel valued if they are allowed to use their preferred styles in some situations.
4. The more people are allowed to use their preferred styles, the more energy they can have to achieve team goals.

Attachment A: Style Profile Sheet with Descriptions

Direct _____ Indirect_____ Storytelling

Low Context _____ High Context

Faster Pace_____ Slower Pace

Formal_____ Informal

Detached _____ Attached _____Intuitive

Communications Style Continua

While each individual may use multiple styles, there are identifiable, culturally taught preferences. Use of multiple styles is common although there tends to be a personal preference that is the style individuals may revert to under pressure. Misperceptions and/or conflict is common when individuals are using different styles. Style refers to *how* one speaks, not *what* one says.

DIRECT:

- What one means is stated in a straightforward, direct manner. No "beating around the bush."
- Directness is equated with honesty and respect for the other person and the other person's time.
- Supports the values of saving time and focusing on task.

INDIRECT:

- Meaning is conveyed by subtle means such as nonverbal behaviors, questions, stories, parables, or use of a third party.
- Indirectness is equated with politeness and respect for the other person and the other person's feelings.
- Supports the values of relationship, history, and group harmony.

STORYTELLING:

- Meaning is conveyed through stories or parables.
- Stories are equated with allowing others to decide the meaning for themselves.
- Supports the values of relationship, history, and group meaning.

LOW CONTEXT:

- The context of communication is not assumed to be known. Things must be explained clearly and unambiguously.
- Tends to use lots of words because the words establish the context/meaning.
- Supports providing detail and information to avoid misunderstanding.

HIGH CONTEXT:

- The context of communication is assumed to be known. It is unnecessary, even disrespectful, to explain things precisely.
- Tends to use few words because the context establishes the meaning.
- Leave understanding to the other person and respect their understanding of the situation.

FASTER PACED:

- Speech patterns are rapid, indicating engagement and intelligence.
- Expect answers to questions immediately.
- Risk is eliminating participation by people whose culture has taught a more reflective, slower pace; those who have some forms of disability (e.g., hearing loss), and those for whom English is a second language.

SLOWER PACED:

- Speech patterns are slower, indicating reflection and thoughtfulness.
- Responses to questions expected after the other person has time to reflect; not immediate.

FORMAL:

- Communication is governed by strict rules regarding such things as forms of address based on age, status, topics.
- Communication is ritualized, including the use of organizational hierarchy to determine who can/cannot be talked to and under what circumstances.
- Supports the values of status and hierarchy.

INFORMAL:

- Communication has few rules; people tend to be addressed by first name.
- Communication is less bound to specific conventions. More flexibility in what is said, to whom one can speak, and under what circumstances.
- Supports the values of fairness and equity.

DETACHED:

- Focus is on objective information/data and tends to be linear.
- The emphasis is on ideas that are separate from the person. Disagreement with another person's ideas is acceptable and even valued. It is not seen as a personal attack.
- Listen carefully to the ideas; if you disagree say so—the disagreement is with the idea, not the person.
- Preference in discussion is to remain objective and not personalize—indicates objectivity and fairness.
- Preference for "taking turns" when talking.
- Information generally presented in a linear manner.
- Less comfortable with feeling discussions.
- Less variation in tone or gestures.
- When announcing a decision, focuses on facts or information.
- To be effective be brief, state the point, and avoid lengthy explanations.

ATTACHED:

- Focus is on feelings. Tend to appear more people-oriented and passionate . Communication may be more circular.
- The emphasis is on the person, so great importance is attached to feelings. Issues, ideas, and the person are not separate. Disagreement, if done at all, is done carefully and often indirectly because the person and idea are not separate—disagreement with ideas is an attack on the person.
- Sharing one's values and feelings about the issues is highly valued—indicates personal investment.
- Can overlap (interrupt) when others are speaking.
- Generally can hear feeling in the voice regardless of volume.
- May present information in a more circular manner.
- The point may be left unstated because the verbal and nonverbal information is sufficient for understanding; stating the point explicitly may be seen as disrespectful.
- Prefer to involve people and aim for consensus.
- Greater variation in tone and gestures.
- When announcing a decision may describe it in terms of how it will affect people, relationships, or morale.
- To be effective, use stories, allow time for embellishment

INTUITIVE:

- Focus on "knowing" based on experience. The connection between knowing and experience is often not conscious.
- Discussion is more internal with self than external with others.
- Process is less linear, and less conscious, and more difficult to describe to others.
- Increased experience may lead to more rapid decisions although the process for getting there is neither conscious nor subject to justification.
- Prefers more reflection to identify the "knowing" than external discussion.
- When announcing a decision, typically just gives the decision without justification.

SOURCES:

Condon, J. C., and F. Yousef. (1975). *An Introduction to Intercultural Communication*. New York: MacMillan.

Kim, Y. Y. (1986). *Interethnic Communication*. Newbury Park, CA: Sage Publications.

Nelson, G. L., M. A. Batal, and E. B. Yaguida. (2002). Directness vs. indirectness: Egyptian Arabic and US English communication style. *International Journal of Intercultural Relations, 26*, 39–57.

Saphiere, Dianne Hofner, Barbara Kappler Mikk, and Basma Ibrahim DeVries. (2005). *Communication Highwire: Leveraging the Power of Diverse Communication Style*. Yarmouth, ME: Intercultural Press.

Attachment B: Style Profile Sheet

Direct _____ Indirect _____ Storytelling

Low Context _____High Context

Faster Pace_____ Slower Pace

Formal_____ Informal

Detached _____ Attached _____Intuitive

Note: One of these to be enlarged to 18 × 24 inches for each table of 4–6 participants.

22

Bridging Behaviors

Time Required:

45 minutes: 15 minutes for lecture, 15 minutes for activity, 15 minutes to debrief

Objectives:

To help participants:

1. Practice using techniques for clarifying the other person's behaviors.
2. Practice identifying positive intentions in behaviors that may not feel positive to the receiver.

Materials:

Situations that have relevance to the participants (see samples on page 101)

Process:

1. Using one of the samples on page 101, provide an interactive lecture that focuses on techniques that create an opportunity for positive communication when someone else's behavior has had a negative impact on you:
   a. Assume the other person has positive intent.
   b. Generate as many possible explanations for the behavior as possible.
   c. Seek clarification by stating your intent (e.g., I want to understand your intention so we can work more effectively together).
   d. Describe the other person's behavior and ask them to interpret it, that is to share their intention.
2. Place participants in groups of 3–4 and provide each group with 3–5 situations. Allow 15 minutes for the discussion.
3. Ask each small group to report the intentions they identified for the behavior and its statement of intention in seeking clarification for *one* of the situations it was given.

Debriefing Questions:

1. How did you feel about looking for a positive explanation for these behaviors?
2. What situations were easiest to identify positive explanations for? Which were hardest? Why?
3. What implications does this process have for you on a daily basis at work/school, or in your personal life?

Debriefing Conclusions:

1. When we see, or experience, someone else's behavior that is different from what we would do in a similar situation, we often jump to a negative evaluation.
2. Most people act with good intentions but the impact on others can often be negative.
3. Seeking clarification about the reason someone else does something can help us understand them—and their behavior—better.
4. Understanding why someone does something can often allow us to either (a) accept the behavior or (b) suggest alternative behaviors with a more positive attitude.

Sample Situations

1. You have a new coworker (or manager) to whom you have been introduced. Virtually every morning for the first week she has been at the organization, you pass her in the hallway in the morning and greet her with a friendly "good morning." She does not return your greeting—nor does she acknowledge you in any way including with eye contact.

2. You are standing outside of a room where some of your colleagues are joking around when you hear them tell a joke that you perceive to be offensive and all of them laugh. You are offended—and surprised because you would not have expected this of them.

3. Your manager (or teacher) consistently gives you "corrective feedback" but never tells you when you are doing a good job.

4. Your manager (or teacher) gives you an assignment with no specific information about how to accomplish it.

5. Your manager (or teacher) gives you an assignment with such specific instructions about how to accomplish it that there is no opportunity for you to demonstrate creativity or use your own skills and experience.

6. You are a new employee (or student) and notice that a group of people go out for drinks or lunch together very regularly and you are never invited.

7. You have lead a team that has completed a very important project and your manager tells you it is brilliant and she will be presenting it at a major conference. You attend the conference with her and listen to her report about the project during which she makes no mention of your critical role in its completion.

8. You are the only female on a project team. The team leader has consistently refused to meet with you alone—insisting that every time you want to talk with him, another member of the team should be present.

9. You are a female who has a new male coworker who persistently stands close enough to touch your arm or shoulder as you talk.

10. You are newly employed in a country whose language is not your first language. You are relatively fluent but still struggle with some of the more technical language of your organization. Your manager persistently completes your sentences when you hesitate to think about the proper phrase for what you want to say.

23

The Intercultural Classroom

Time Required:

90 minutes: 20 minutes for lecture regarding styles, 5 minutes setting up the video exercise, 20 minute video, 15 minutes for small group exercise, 30 minutes for debriefing

Objectives:

To help participants:

1. Identify a series of cultural communication style continua.
2. Identify the methods for being most effective in communicating with people using each of those styles.
3. Practice identifying the styles being used by speakers in a video.

Materials:

Video: *A Different Place: The Intercultural Classroom*[1]

Description of Communication Styles Continua for each participant (Attachment A)

List of characters in the video for each participant (Attachment B, first column only)

Process:

1. After reminding people about the differences of generalizations and stereotypes and the power of perception, conduct a brief lecture regarding the communication styles continua including asking participants how someone using one style might perceive someone using the opposite style.
2. Provide each of the participants with a list of the characters in the video and tell them they will be asked to identify which style each character is using after they watch the video.

> **HIGHER**
> **EDUCATION**
> **WORKPLACE**
> **VERBAL**
> **NONVERBAL**
> **M–H**

---

[1] This video has been developed by Dr. Jaime Wurzel and can be accessed for a fee via the Web, or purchased in Video or DVD formats from www. irc-international.com.

Caution that the styles they will observe are extreme for the purpose of observation and discussion and should not be used to stereotype everyone from a given culture because there are many individual differences. Nonetheless, the styles are highly normed in the cultures they are representing. Indicate they can take notes if they wish. Show the video

3. Place participants in small groups of 3–5 people and ask them to identify which style each character used.

4. Regather into the large group and ask small groups to report what style they have decided each character was using. Challenge groups to give reasons for their decisions. Where groups disagree, discuss why.

5. Referring back to the communication styles continua handout, discuss the behaviors that can be most effective in working with each style.

6. Debrief.

Debriefing Questions:

1. What part of this exercise was most difficult? Why? What was easiest? Why?

2. What insights did you gain about communication styles and the challenges you might have communicating with someone from a different cultural style?

3. How can you apply this information to your daily life?

Debriefing Conclusions:

1. Cultures teach specific ways to communicate—and some of those ways are totally opposite from each other—which can affect perceptions across communication style differences.

2. Being able to identify the style someone is using and how to adapt for that style can lead to more effective communication.

Optional way to conduct the exercise:

Participants can be divided into small groups of 3–5 before showing the video, with each small group assigned one or two of the characters so they can focus more clearly on observing one or two characters rather than all of them.

Adapted with permission from an exercise created by Dr. Janet Bennett and Dr. Milton Bennett.

Attachment A: Communication Styles Continua

LINEAR	CIRCULAR
Communication is conducted in a straight line, moving in a linear way toward the main point. "Getting to the point" is very important and the point is stated explicitly. Not getting to the point quickly is seen as a time waster.	Communication is conducted in a circular manner around the main point. The point may be left unstated because the verbal and nonverbal information provided is sufficient for understanding. Stating the point explicitly is seen as insulting to the other person.
• Be brief. • Preface your remarks with "the point is . . ." • Provide only as much explanation as the other person needs. • Be explicit about the main point. • Do not deviate from the main point.	• Be elegant and flowing with your remarks. • Never preface a comment with "the point is . . ." • Embellish your remarks with stories and anecdotes. Let the story make the point. • Let the other person infer the meaning of your comments from the story.

DIRECT	INDIRECT
What one means is stated in a very straightforward and direct manner. There is no "beating around the bush." Directness is equated with honesty and respect for the other person.	Meaning is conveyed by subtle means such as nonverbal behavior, parables and stories, suggestions and implication. Indirectness is equated with politeness and respect for the other person.
• Respect the other person's time. • Don't create ambiguity or uncertainty by avoiding the issue. • Be straightforward.	• Respect the other person's feelings. • Don't put the other person on the spot by being too direct. • Be polite.

LOW CONTEXT	HIGH CONTEXT
The context of the communication is *not* assumed to be known. Things must be explained clearly and unambiguously. Meaning must be expressed precisely.	The context for communication is assumed to be known. Hence it is unnecessary, even insulting to explain things and state meaning precisely. Meaning is taken from context.
• Always communicate clearly, completely, and unambiguously. • Don't leave understanding to chance.	• Always respect the other person's understanding of the situation. • Leave understanding up to the other person.

ATTACHED (EMOTIONAL)	DETACHED (UNEMOTIONAL)
Communication is carried out with feeling and emotion. Issues are discussed with passion and commitment. Communication is very expressive. Sharing one's values and feelings about the issues is highly valued.	Communication is carried out in a calm and impersonal manner. This is equated with objectivity, which is valued. Highly expressive, emotional, and engaged communication is inappropriate because this is seen as personalizing the issues and as biased.

• State your views with passion and conviction. • If you care about an idea, show it. • Bring yourself as a person into the discussion and show who you are.	• State your views dispassionately. • Avoid being overly emotional. • Avoid personalizing the discussion—keep yourself out of it.
IDEA-FOCUSED	**PERSON-FOCUSED**
The emphasis is on ideas that are seen as separate from the person. Thus, disagreement with another person's ideas is acceptable and even valued. It is not seen as a personal attack. • Listen carefully to the ideas being discussed. • If you disagree with someone's idea, say so. • Because a person's ideas are wrong doesn't mean there is something wrong with the person.	**The emphasis is on the person, hence great importance is attached to the feelings of the other person. Issues and ideas *are not* separated from the person. Thus, disagreement with someone's ideas must be handled very carefully.** • Respond to the person. Be attentive to feelings. • In your communication, be careful not to hurt the other person's feelings. • Understand that an attack on someone's idea is an attack on that person.
TASK-FOCUSED	**RELATIONSHIP-FOCUSED**
Communication focuses on the task at hand and getting it done. The other person's feelings are secondary. Group harmony is secondary to task completion. • Keep focusing on the task at hand. • Don't allow too much small talk to sidetrack the task. • Clarify the task. • Publicly sanction slackards.	**Communication is focused on relationships. Maintaining group harmony is central. The task is secondary. Task completion must not come at the expense of the group or person.** • Make certain that your concern with the task doesn't come at the expense of someone's feelings and the well-being of the group. • Praise the participants for their good work. • Never publicly call down a colleague.
FORMAL	**INFORMAL**
Communication is governed by strict rules regarding such things as forms of address, ways to address persons of different age and status, topics that can and cannot be discussed, and so on. Communication in many respects is highly ritualized. • Study the rules of communication in the target society and follow them.	**Communication is less bound to specific conventions. Persons have more flexibility in what they say, to whom they say it, and under what circumstances. Informal communication might also be demonstrated by the use of the first name, for example.** • Try to find out what is allowable in the host society and follow the conventions.

Adapted from work by Dr. Janet Bennett and Dr. Milton Bennett, 1993. Modified by Dr. Michael Paige, 1996.

Attachment B: The Intercultural Classroom—Characters

Professor Larry Ford (United States)	Linear, Direct, Emotionally Restrained, Intellectually Confrontive
Katja (Russia)	Linear, Direct, Emotionally Expressive, Intellectually Confrontive
Simon (South Africa)	Circular, Indirect, Emotionally Restrained, No Confrontation
Esteban (El Salvador)	Circular, Direct, Emotionally Expressive, Relationally Confrontive
Ming (China)	Circular, Indirect, Emotionally Restrained, No Confrontation
Mariko (Japan)	Circular, Indirect, Emotionally Restrained, No Confrontation
Charlie (United States)	Linear, Direct, Emotionally Restrained—at least trying to be, Relationally Confrontive
Amy (United States)	Linear, Direct, Emotionally Restrained, Relationally Confrontive
Joanna (United States)	Linear, Direct, Emotionally Expressive, Relationally Confrontive

Note: The right hand column indicating each character's styles should be removed when preparing participant handouts.

Adapted with permission from an exercise created by Dr. Janet Bennett and Dr Milton Bennett.

24

What's in a Word ?

Time Required:

45 minutes: 10 minutes to introduce the exercise, 10 minutes in small groups, 10 minutes to report small group results, 15 minutes to debrief

Objectives:

1. To demonstrate the importance of being specific about words we often assume everyone defines the same way.
2. To demonstrate the power of using specific behavioral definitions of key words.
3. To help participants identify the importance of specificity in communication in order to create an inclusive environment where each individual has an equal opportunity for success.

Materials:

Flip charts

Markers

Process:

1. Provide a brief lecture:
   - Identify the importance of providing rules for success when new individuals enter a team.
   - Ask the group what rules exist in their team. Record the rules on a flip chart.
   - Select one or two "rules" and ask people to define those rules with specific behaviors. For example, if a rule is that people are expected to be respectful, ask them to identify specific behaviors that would be considered respectful.
   - Give one or two examples of cultural differences in how "rules" are defined. For example, one person may believe respect is demonstrated by direct eye contact while another may believe respect is demonstrated by avoiding eye contact.

If one of these people is a newcomer to a team and is merely told that team members are expected to be respectful, they may exhibit a form of eye contact that is considered disrespectful to others while they are intending to demonstrate respect.

- Conclude with the point that the more behavioral we are in communicating expectations, the more likely others are to be successful in meeting those expectations.

2. Place people in teams of 4–5 and give them 10 minutes to identify as many behaviors as possible that indicate someone is a good team member. Caution them to be both behavioral and specific. For example, a good team member shows respect by not interrupting others when they are talking. *Not:* a good team member shows respect for others.

3. Ask each small group to report their behaviors, which should be recorded on easel paper. Listen carefully to be sure that each item is really a behavior, not a concept.

4. After each small group has reported its behaviors, look for areas where there is agreement and areas where there could be conflict.

Debriefing Questions:

1. What was most challenging about this exercise?
2. What insights or reminders did you get from this experience?
3. What implications does this have for your organization? Your team? You personally?

Debriefing Conclusions:

1. Using specific behavioral terms when communicating is a key strategy for avoiding misunderstanding.
2. The greater the cultural differences between those communicating, the more critical behavioral terms are for avoiding miscommunication.

Pacing

Time Required:

30 minutes: 10 for pacing lecture, 5 for conversation, 15 for debriefing.

WORKPLACE
EDUCATION
NONVERBAL
L

Objectives:

To help participants identify:

1. Three primary patterns of communication pacing.
2. How people using different pacing patterns might perceive one another.
3. Effective ways to manage pacing patterns.

Materials:

Pacing Narrative (Attachment)

Process:

1. Provide information about different pacing patterns using the Pacing Narrative.
2. Place participants in groups of 3. Assign each person in each triad a different pacing pattern and give them 5 minutes to conduct a conversation on any topic relevant to the group.
3. Debrief the experience.

Debriefing Questions:

1. What happened during this conversation?
    a. How did you feel?
    b. What did you do?
2. What specific strategies could you use if different pacing patterns existed in conversations with others?

Debriefing Conclusions:

1. When people are using different pacing patterns they can misperceive one another.

2. Recognizing different pacing patterns can help manage both the conversation and the misperceptions.
3. Verbalizing the different patterns you recognize and asking for an agreement about how the conversation can proceed will create a more effective cross-cultural conversation.

Attachment : Pacing Narrative

There are three basic pacing patterns people use when communicating.

- This first pattern is most often used by detached and more fast-paced communicators. This could also be called "take turns" talking. When we are conversing I listen for the period at the end of your sentence. Visually, it might look like:

Person A	Person B	Person A	Person B

- The second pattern is used by people who are from more reflective or slower-paced communication style cultures. When I hear the period at the end of your sentence, then and only then do I begin reflecting on what you have said and how I want to respond. It would be inconceivable for me to begin preparing a response before you had finished because I don't have all of your information yet. That means there will be a pause between when you finish talking and when I begin talking. If you are using the same pacing pattern, you will be fine with the silence created by my reflection. If, on the other hand, you are using the "take turns" pacing pattern, you might interrupt my silence and respond for me—often thinking you are doing me a favor because I "don't have an answer." This can be perceived as rude by the reflective pacing pattern and can result in the more reflective pattern never being heard. Visually, it might look like:

Person A	Person B	Person A

- The third pattern is one more often seen in attached or faster-paced communicators. In this pattern, I jump into the middle of your sentence; you jump into mine, and so on. Sometimes we are both talking simultaneously, leaving those who are using the other two pacing patterns wondering if we ever listen to each other. There are two types of this pattern: interruptive and overlapping. The difference is in the content. If I jump into your sentence and change the subject, become the expert, or take the conversation away from you, it is an interruptive pattern. If, on the other hand, I jump into your sentence to agree, support what you are saying, ask for more information, and don't change the subject, it is likely an overlapping pattern. Visually, this pattern might look like:

Person A	Person A	Person A

Person B	Person B	Person B

If you tend to use one of the top two patterns, you might find the last one challenging—it is most often felt to be an interruption. If you are able, however, to listen for the content it can be helpful. If you identify someone who is simply overlapping you may be able to allow them to continue doing so—they are, after all, intending to be supportive. If, on the other hand, what they are doing is really interruptive, you may then wish to ask that they wait until you have completed your thoughts before they speak.

The challenge is not with any of these patterns specifically. Rather, the challenge is when two different people are using two different patterns and misperceive each other.

26

Switching Directions: Direct/Indirect

Time Required:

45 minutes: 10 minutes for lecture, 20 minutes for small group exercise, 15 minutes to debrief

Objectives:

To help participants:

1. Identify how people using direct and indirect communication styles can misperceive one another.
2. Practice switching statements from direct to indirect and from indirect to direct.

Materials:

A series of Direct and Indirect statements (samples in Attachment A)

Process:

1. Give the following brief lecture:
   Cultures teach their members to communicate in a more direct way or a more indirect way. Generally speaking, people from Western cultures communicate in a direct, explicit manner. The meaning is on the surface, and a listener doesn't have to know much about the context or the speaker to understand. (Note that there are, of course, individual differences in every culture and caution against using this information to stereotype any individual. Rather, encourage participants to listen to how others talk in order to determine if they are using a direct or indirect communication style.)

   People from other cultures communicate in a more indirect manner. Generally speaking, this tends to apply to non-Western cultures. Messages are transmitted through stories, analogies, questions, third parties, or nonverbal behaviors.

An indirect communicator is usually able to understand a direct message, although the communicator may be perceived as abrupt or rude. On the other hand, the direct communicator tends to have more difficulty understanding an indirect message and may perceive the indirect communicator as vague or indecisive.

Cross-cultural competency requires that individuals (a) first understand their own style preference; (b) are able to listen to other styles effectively and without negative judgment; and (c) utilize other styles.

(Ask people to talk a little bit about which style they prefer, with which one they have the greatest challenge, where they are encountering their most challenging style, and so on.)

2. Tell participants they are going to practice taking direct statements and turning them into indirect statements and vice versa.

3. Place people in groups of 3–5 and give each group several statements. Ask them to (a) identify if the statement is direct or indirect and then (b) as a group, identify a way to reverse the statement. That is, make direct statements indirect and make indirect statements direct. (There are sample statements in the Attachment but you should encourage people to bring their own—and you should bring statements you have heard in this particular work or educational environment over the past few days.)

4. Debrief in the large group.

Debriefing Questions:

1. What was easiest or hardest about this exercise? Why?
2. How did you feel while doing it?
3. How can this information and experience help you as you communicate with others who are different from you culturally?

Debriefing Conclusions:

1. Direct and indirect communicators can misunderstand or misperceive one another.
2. Learning to hear, and use, both styles will increase one's cross-cultural communication competence.

Attachment A

DIRECT STATEMENTS:

1. I need this completed by tomorrow at 10 A.M.
2. You will need to provide your own equipment if you want to show a video in class.
3. Your office seems very sparse.
4. The information you gave in the nonverbal section of your presentation was wrong.
5. Your management style is very laissez faire, which doesn't encourage growth in your subordinates.
6. I need you to get this project finished by the deadline.
7. If you don't get your homework done you will not complete this class.
8. You need to let me know what type of food you want for the party.
9. You have difficulty arriving on time, don't you?
10. I would like it if you would quit the small talk so we can get a work plan finished.

INDIRECT STATEMENTS:

1. When I worked for Division A they allowed us to establish our own deadlines.
2. The early bird gets the worm.
3. My mother used to tell me that it was important to listen to the whole story before making decisions.
4. The nail that sticks up feels the hammer first.
5. I am not sure . . . what would you like to do?
6. I would like to watch you do that again.
7. Would Tuesday be a good day for that?
8. It may get here tomorrow (in response to an inquiry about a product that is never going to be available).
9. That could be very difficult (in response to an inquiry about whether something can be delivered by a certain date—meaning "no," which would be rude to say).
10. I wonder if people are comfortable with the temperature in here.

Your Choice: Style Continuum

27

Time Required:

80–100 minutes: 50–60 minutes for activity, 30–40 minutes to debrief

Objectives:

To help participants:

1. Explore various communication styles.
2. Identify personal communication preferences.
3. Discuss strengths and challenges of various styles.
4. Experience "style switching."

Materials:

Pens or pencils for participants

Communication Style Continuum Handout

Slide and/or large chart with markers

Process:

1. Briefly describe the various communication styles on handout.
2. Ask participants to complete the style continuum (5–10 minutes).
3. Form small groups of 6–8 participants (even numbers, if possible).
4. Use chart or slide to explain the group assignment:
   a. Share your preferences with the group.
   b. Compare similarities and differences within the group.
   c. Discuss the possible impact of style differences: on individuals, on teams, at the organizational level.
   d. List at least two strengths and two possible challenges for each style.
5. Choose someone in the group whose style differs from yours.
6. Use your *partner's style* to communicate the following scenarios: (allow 15–20 minutes for each partner).

a. It is important to arrive at work on time.

b. There will be no employee bonus check this year.

c. You have done an excellent job.

Debriefing Questions:

1. How did you feel completing your continuum? Sharing with your group? Identifying strengths and challenges?
2. What were some of the similarities or differences within your group?
3. Were there any surprises?
4. How easy was it to switch styles?
5. What did you learn from this activity?
6. How might you use the information from this experience in your personal and/or your professional life?

Debriefing Conclusions:

1. Individuals have a preferred communication style.
2. Each communication style has both strengths and challenges.
3. Understanding communication style preference can enhance communication effectiveness.
4. Switching to the receiver's preferred style can enhance communication effectiveness.

Optional ways to conduct the exercise:

The language of the exercise could be adjusted to either a classroom or business setting. The concepts and objectives could be applied to written (to include e-mail and blogging) as well as verbal communication.

The topics of discussion can be specific to the issues of the organization or work team.

Adapted from an activity by Patricia Cassiday, Collaborative Connection, Seattle, 2008.

Communication Style Continuum Handout

Understanding our own communication preference, while exploring the preferences of others, can be a valuable tool for enhancing our ability to communicate. When there is a mismatch between the intent of our message and the impact on the receiver, a difference in communication style is usually the issue.

Linear: Get to the point, state issue explicitly, wordy communication wastes time

Circular: Use of context (story) to make the point, elegance in language, crass to clearly state point

Direct: State specifics, avoid ambiguity, honesty requires directness

Indirect: Specifically citing a mistake or voicing disapproval is impolite and disrespectful, subtle implication allows for "face-saving"

Formal: Status is important and acknowledged, follow strict communication rules

Informal: Few specific rules on what can be said to whom, use of first names

Detached: Calm, objective, impersonal

Attached: Passionate, strong feelings, personal stake in outcome

Idea Focus: Disagree and attack idea not person, person and idea totally separate

Person Focus: Disagreement is subtle, person/ideas same, feelings important

Task: Accomplishing the goal/task is priority, feelings secondary

Relationship: Group harmony, relations priority, everyone should feel heard

Low Context: Over-explain, many words, specific, precise

High Context: Under-explain, subtle nonverbals, understanding left to the receiver, over-explaining is insulting

---

Adapted from an activity by Patricia Cassiday, Collaborative Connection, Seattle, 2008.

Communication Style Continuum

Please take a few minutes to think about your preferred communication style. Indicate your preference with an X along each of these style continuums.

Linear _____ Circular

Direct _____ Indirect

Formal_____ Informal

Detached _____ Attached

Idea Focus _____ Person Focus

Task_____Relationship

Low Context _____High Context

Adapted from an activity by Patricia Cassiday, Collaborative Connection, Seattle, 2008.

28

Debate or Dialogue?

WORKPLACE
VERBAL
M–H

Time Required:

90 minutes: 10 minutes to set up, Part I: 15 minutes in homogeneous groups, 10 minutes in pairs; Part 2: 15 minutes in homogeneous groups, 10 minutes in pairs, 10 minutes to review handout, 20 minutes to debrief

Objectives:

To help participants:

1. Experience the difference between debate and dialogue.
2. Identify the context in which each is most effective.

Materials:

Debate or Dialogue Handout (Attachment A)

Sample Topic List (Attachment B)

Process:

1. Divide participants into two groups: One labeled "Pro," the other labeled "Con."
2. Assign a topic from the Sample Topic List (Attachment B) or one relevant to the group with which you are working.
3. Give the participants 15 minutes in homogeneous groups (Pros together, Cons together) to identify all possible points they can make to persuade the other side that they are right.
4. Partner each Pro participant with a Con participant and give them 10 minutes together with the instruction that their task is to persuade the other person that they are correct.
5. After 10 minutes, give the group a second topic for discussion.
6. Give the participants 15 minutes in homogeneous groups (Pros together, Cons together) to identify all possible points they can share about their position.
7. Partner each Pro participant with the same Con participant they were with before and give them 10 minutes together with

the instruction that their task is to listen carefully, trying to understand the position of the other participant and to identify common points of agreement.

8. Distribute the Debate or Dialogue Handout and allow time for participants to read the information before debriefing.

Debriefing Questions:

1. How would you compare your feelings in the first and second conversations?
2. Under what circumstances have you experienced each of these forms of conversation? With what outcome?
3. How could these two different approaches affect cross-cultural communication?
4. When would it be advantageous to facilitate a debate, a discussion, or a dialogue?
5. Where and when could you use this information in your current organization?

Debriefing Conclusions:

1. A debate transpires when we are seeking, or assume there is, one right answer, which can limit our perspective.
2. Debate "listening" focuses on: inaccuracies, miscalculations, errors from the opponent to use as counterarguments.
3. A dialogue transpires when we seek multiple possibilities, a variety of new options, or perspectives.
4. Dialogue "listening" focuses on: shared understanding, unique perspectives, creative approaches, multiple solutions.
5. Effective cross-cultural communication tends to be enhanced through dialogue.

Optional ways to conduct the exercise:

It is important to ensure a safe climate and foundation of trust before proceeding with "conflict-laden" topics. If the topic is high risk, be sure to allow additional time for debriefing. Debate/Dialogue topics, specific to an organization, or work team, especially during a merger or acquisition, can be volatile. If you are a new trainer working alone it may be best to select topics unrelated to the specific work setting.

Attachment A: Debate or Dialogue Handout

The communication techniques of debate and dialogue differ in desired goal and basic approach. Determine your ultimate communication goal or desired outcome. When you are clear about what you hope to accomplish, you will be able to choose the most effective way to approach the communication.

DEBATE	DIALOGUE
Goal: Single Resolution	Goal: Multiple Options/Common Ground
Clarify differences	Discover common ground
Identify specifics	Generate options
Affirm a point of view	Explore diverse perspectives
Work competitively	Work collaboratively
Seek conclusion/closure	Seeks multiple possibilities/open ended
Challenge thinking	Expands thinking
Find the "best" solution	Find multiple solutions
Listen for flaws in others' position	Listen for strength in others' position
Narrow choice (either/or)	Expand choices
Accomplish task	Build on relationship

© Patricia Cassiday, Collaborative Connection, Seattle, 2008.

Attachment B: Sample Topic List

1. The world would be safer if only law enforcement agents could own guns legally.
2. Anyone entering the country illegally should be deported without exception.
3. Offshore drilling should be eliminated immediately.
4. Global warming is a myth created to support Al Gore.
5. Socialized medicine is the only way to have equity in health care.
6. Surveillance should be permitted without a court order if national security is at stake.
7. Women's right to choose should be without question.
8. Gay marriage should be determined by popular vote.
9. Nongrading education systems produce nonthinking adults.
10. Corporate monopoly should be allowed.
11. People not using public transportation should pay higher transportation taxes for the damage done by their vehicles.
12. Military draft should be reinstituted.
13. Schools should operate year round.
14. Alternative energy should receive all research and development monies from the federal government.
15. (Current topics from local news.)

29

First Impressions

Time Required:

35–45 minutes: 15–25 minutes for activity, 20 minutes for debrief

Objectives:

1. To implement group icebreaker.
2. To help participants experience the power of nonverbal communication.
3. To help participants explore gender and cultural differences in nonverbal communication.
4. To expand participants' awareness of nonverbal patterns.

Materials:

Communication pattern cards (color coded by gender; see page 129)

Timer or clock

Process:

1. Explain that this icebreaker activity consists of 3–5 rounds of introductions (allow 4–5 minutes for each round, depending on group size).
2. Ask participants to draw a card describing a communication pattern. Tell them to exaggerate the communication pattern during the introduction.
3. Have the participants elect a person of the opposite gender whenever possible. Each should introduce self and share information about career, hobby, and/or family as is comfortable.
4. Debrief the experience discussing first impressions.

Debriefing Questions:

1. What did you think when you read your card? Was this a familiar pattern for you? Similar to your experience? Were there any special personal challenges?

2. How did you feel meeting someone new? Were you able to "stay in character"? How did the other person handle the experience?
3. Were there any surprises during this activity? Did you learn something new?
4. How might you use this experience in the future?

Debriefing Conclusions:

1. Nonverbal behavior has a major impact on what is communicated.
2. Many nonverbal behaviors are gender and/or culturally specific.
3. Effective communication is enhanced by expanding awareness of nonverbal patterns.

Adapted from an activity by Patricia Cassiday, Collaborative Connection, Seattle, 2008.

Communication Pattern Cards

Place these patterns on individual 4 × 6 index cards. Each gender will be a different color code. You can use colored cards or indicate the gender using colored dots or markers.

MALE CARDS

You will be promoting the "smiley-face syndrome." Throughout your introduction, when you are speaking and when you are listening, you should be sure to have a happy smile.

You are a very expressive person; your personality seems to "bubble over." Please exaggerate your enthusiasm when introducing yourself and when learning about the other person.

Eyes are powerful communicators. For this exercise, you will be avoiding eye contact and exaggerating blinking. During your introduction and during the time you are learning about the other person, you will be looking down, looking around the room, and blinking frequently.

Hands are communication transmitters. During this exercise you will exaggerate your hands by twisting your rings and rubbing your hands together through the introduction of yourself and even more so when learning about the other person.

Personal space communicates differently across gender and culture. For this exercise you are going to maintain approximately 16″ between you and the person you are meeting. If the other person backs up, you will move forward.

FEMALE CARDS

This is serious business and you are going to exaggerate that in your introduction. When you introduce yourself and when you are listening to the other person's introduction, your face must express your serious approach. You must not smile at any time during this exercise.

During the introductions, you will demonstrate that you are powerful and entitled to due respect. You must keep all emotions in check. Do not reveal any feelings or emotional response during your introduction or when receiving information from the other participant.

Our eyes are powerful communicators. If you have sunglasses with you, wear them throughout the exercise. If you do not have sunglasses, let your eye contact wander off when your partner is talking. Exaggerate your "disinterest" frequently.

Hands are communication transmitters. During this exercise you will exaggerate your hands by rubbing your chin in a pensive way indicating that you are "thinking or judging." Do this even more so when learning about the other person.

Personal space communicates differently across gender and culture. For this exercise you are going to maintain approximately 36" between you and the person you are meeting. If the other person moves forward, you will move back.

Adapted from an activity by Patricia Cassiday, Collaborative Connection, Seattle, 2008.

30

Sounds Like Silence

Time Required:

40–60 minutes: 20–30 minutes for activity, 20–30 minutes for debrief

Objectives:

To help participants:

1. Explore multiple meanings of silence.
2. Experience silence in person-to-person communication.
3. Develop a degree of comfort with silence as a communication tool.

Materials:

Sounds Like Silence Handout

Timer or watch

Process:

1. Distribute the Sounds Like Silence Handout and give participants time to review it.
2. Have participants choose a partner (preferably someone they do not know).
3. Briefly describe the activity.
4. **Round I:** Introduce a "value neutral" topic such as travel (favorite place, how to get there, special activities, food, music, art, etc.). Allow 1–2 minutes for participants to gather thoughts.
   - Person A takes the lead, speaking for 3–4 minutes about travel. (Person A is asked to build in at least three 15-second periods of silence.)
   - The listener, Person B, then provides feedback on what they heard from Person A and how they felt during the silence.
   - Person B then speaks for 3–4 minutes with at least three 15-second periods of silence.

- The listener, Person A, then provides feedback on what they heard from Person B. and how they he felt during the silence.

5. **Round II:** Repeat this same process with a topic that is not value neutral, such as gun control, immigration, global warming, and so on. The topic may be specifically related to different priorities within the organization or related to the training. Debrief with whole group

Debriefing Questions:

1. How did you feel during the conversations? Talking? Listening?
2. What impact did silence have on the communication? On the meaning or impact of the message?
3. Were there differences between the first round and the second round? Was it more difficult to maintain the silence? Why might differences occur?
4. What advice would you give to someone who was going to participate in this activity? Meeting someone from another country?
5. How might you use information about silence in your life?

Debriefing Conclusions:

1. Silence is a powerful communication tool.
2. Silence can prevent communication or improve communication.
3. Silence can provide "thinking" time for the speaker and/or add emphasis and meaning.
4. Silence can be used to create personal distance or power imbalance in a relationship.
5. In some cultures silence is highly valued, conveying a sense of respect, trust, and meaning.
6. In some cultures silence can be a signal of approval or disapproval.
7. In some cultures silence can be viewed as an admission of guilt.
8. Understanding the various uses of silence can improve our clarity in communication.

Optional ways to conduct the exercises:

The level of risk can be altered by the selection of topics. In a multicultural setting, topics of diversity or communication style can be introduced.

If participants are comfortable with the use of silence (e.g., people from many Asian cultures) the exercise can be switched to communication without any silence. The experience should encourage participants to communicate in a new way using the information from the handout.

Adapted from an activity by Patricia Cassiday, Collaborative Connection, Seattle, 2008.

Sounds of Silence Handout

Silence is an important part of communication that serves many purposes. The tacit meaning of silence is frequently the basis for miscommunication between people from different cultures. It is important to be comfortable with the silence and to be able to interpret its meaning within the context and framework of the conversation.

Here are a few points to keep in mind about the meaning of silence:

1. *"Turn taking"*: Silence can be a signal for "turn taking." The pacing of silence differs from culture to culture. (*Note: Westerners tend to be less comfortable with silence and may "jump in" at the pause, when the speaker has not yet completed his or her thought.*)

2. *Listening:* Silence can be used to create a space for listening. A good listener can create the space for sharing important ideas or experiences. The speaker may also use silence to gather his or her own thoughts before proceeding.

3. *Emphasis:* Silence can be used to emphasize an important point or idea.

4. *Respect:* Silence can indicate respect for a person's status, position, or age. (In some cultures a younger person or person of lesser status may be waiting for an invitation to speak.)

5. *Pressure:* Discomfort with silence can create "pressure" for the listener to "fill the void." This can be used as a technique, leading to unintended disclosure of information (especially true in Western cultures).

6. *Conflict:* Silence may be a "learned behavior" used to deal with conflict. The individual feels anger/rage but cannot or chooses not to find the words to express the feelings.

7. *Ignoring:* Silence can indicate disinterest in the topic and/or the person. Refusing to reply can be a "power play." Silence can be hurtful when used to create personal distance and/or to ignore someone trying to communicate.

8. *Contemplation:* Silence can be an opportunity for the listener to reflect on the situation. Cultures that value introspection draw on silence prior to taking a position on matters of importance.

9. *Therapeutic:* Silence can be therapeutic, providing a safe space for the sharing of a story. This is especially true following situations of crisis and/or trauma. Listening to the experience of the speaker indicates empathy and provides a sense of caring.

10. *Ma:* In Japanese culture it is extremely important to pay attention to "context" to understand the message being communicated. The use of silence (Ma) can indicate messages ranging from respect to tactful disagreement. (The many subtle differences in the use of silence may require clarification from a native speaker.)

11. *Guilt:* Silence can be interpreted as an admission of guilt. This is especially true in Western cultures where words are highly valued. A lack of words can indicate something is being "covered-up."

Adapted from an activity by Patricia Cassiday, Collaborative Connection, Seattle, 2008.

31

Me, Myself, and E-mail

Time Required:

50 minutes: 10 minutes introduction, 20 minutes for activity, 20 minutes to debrief

Objectives:

To help participants:

1. Discuss impact of e-mail on communication.
2. Explore differences in preferred style/form.
3. Compare intent and impact in e-mail.
4. Enhance electronic communication effectiveness.

Materials:

Post-it notes

Pen/pencil for each participant

Chart paper or designated area for posting

Process:

1. Introduce the topic with a brief discussion about sheer volume and time consumed by e-mail. Include anecdotal comments (e.g., "I thought you were taller in your e-mail." "I was sure you had red hair." Private thoughts: "Gee she is always shouting. Someone should tell her to lay off the capitals." "Oh no, an e-mail from Joe: it will take 20 minutes to sort out what he is trying to say.")
2. Have participants work in small groups (4–6). Mix groups to include age, gender, and national cultural diversity. If appropriate, you could also mix groups across organizational divisions or regions.
3. Ask each group to discuss their "pet peeves" in electronic communication. Ask the group to come to consensus on their top five pet peeves and list them on individual Post-it notes.

4. Have each group discuss characteristics of effective e-mail style and generate five Post-it notes for effectiveness.
5. Post the team choices in the designated area for "Pet Peeves" and for "Effective E-mail." Ask participants to cluster the similar issues that have come from different groups on both charts.
6. Ask a volunteer to read both charts. Debrief Pet Peeves/Effective E-mail with the large group.

Debriefing Questions:

1. Are there common themes in e-mail annoyances? Similarities or patterns in positive solutions?
2. What did you learn during the small group discussion? Were there any surprises in your group?
3. What differences did you find in your group? Were there any that could be attributed to age, gender, nationality, or other demographic differences? How did you manage those differences?
4. What did you learn about your own e-mail preferences?
5. How can you use this information personally? Organizationally?

Debriefing Conclusions:

1. E-mail volume, speed, and purpose impacts our daily lives.
2. Electronic communication can be enhanced by clear, concise messages. Agreement about a standard writing protocol and what constitutes a respectful style (e.g., greeting, length, content) will reduce negative impact and lead to more effective communication.
3. "Reply to all" should be used with discretion.
4. Tone and/or nuance cannot be easily conveyed electronically.
5. Being aware of age, gender, nationality, or occupational differences can enhance electronic communication.
6. Electronic communication should never be used to deliver difficult messages (e.g., performance feedback).

Adapted from an activity by Patricia Cassiday, Collaborative Connection, Seattle, 2008.

32

High Road, Low Road

Time Required:

45 minutes: 10 minutes to define High and Low Context Communication, 10 minutes for small group preparation, 10 minutes for two presentations. 15 minutes to debrief

Objectives:

To help participants:

1. Understand the difference between high and low context communication styles.
2. Experience the potential misunderstanding that can occur when a high context and a low context communicator try to communicate.
3. Identify tools for avoiding misunderstanding between high and low context communicators.

Materials:

Definitions of high and low context communication (Attachment A)

4 sets of High/Low Context Group Instructions (Attachment B)

Process:

1. Define high and low context communication (see Attachment A). Give an example of each in the context of the organization in which you are conducting the exercise.
2. Divide the group into four teams.
3. One group is called High Group Presenters; one is called High Group Receivers; one group is called Low Group Presenters; one is called Low Group Receivers. Give each team the instructions for their team only.
4. Give the teams 10 minutes to prepare for an interaction using the instructions.

5. Bring the teams back together and allow two rounds of "instructions."
   - **Round 1:** Have the presenter of the Low Context team provide instructions to the receiver of the High Context team.
   - **Round 2:** Have the presenter of the High Context team provide instructions to the receiver of the Low Context team.
6. Debrief the interaction experience.

Debriefing Questions:

1. What was most challenging in preparing for the interaction?
2. What was most challenging during the interaction?
3. What implications could this have for your everyday life?

Debriefing Conclusions:

1. Cultures that are homogeneous and/or whose members have long histories together will often use high context communication. An example of this is acronyms inside of organizations that everyone understands if they have been in the organization a long time.
2. People often assume that others understand what they understand and therefore may not give sufficient detail.
3. Newcomers to a culture are often unintentionally excluded from communication because they don't understand the high context communication.
4. Identifying what someone needs—the level of detail and context—in order to fully understand what is being communicated can create more effective communication and relationships.
5. People often judge others' intentions based on the impact of using different styles.

Attachment A: Definitions of High and Low Context Communication

Low Context

The context of the communication is *not* assumed to be known. Things must be explained clearly and unambiguously. Meaning must be expressed precisely. Often seen as "wordy" or "micromanaging" by high context communicators.

Low context communicators:

- Always communicate clearly, completely, and unambiguously.
- Don't leave understanding to chance.

High Context

The context for communication is assumed to be known. Hence it is unnecessary, even insulting to explain things and state meaning precisely. Meaning is taken from context. Often seen as not giving enough information or direction by low context communicators.

High context communicators:

- Always respect the other person's understanding of the situation.
- Leave understanding up to the other person.

Attachment B: High/Low Context Group Instructions

Low Context Presenter:

As a team, prepare to give someone instructions for a report they are to develop and present to a high-status group (e.g., Board of Directors; School Board, etc.). Select one of your members to deliver the instructions. During the delivery of the instructions, your "presenter" can ask for assistance from the group, or the group can intervene and offer assistance if they feel the presenter is not delivering the message in sufficient low context style. Your receiver may want to interrupt you and get right to the task. Avoid this and continue providing details.

High Context Presenter:

As a team, prepare to tell someone that they need to identify specific information and data in order to effectively complete a project for which they are responsible.

Select one of your members to deliver the instructions. During the delivery of the instructions, your "presenter" can ask for assistance from the group, or the group can intervene and offer assistance if they feel the presenter is not delivering the message in sufficient high context style. Avoid or "skim over" questions the receiver may ask. For example, you might keep repeating "you have the skills necessary to find this information."

Low Context Receivers:

As a team, prepare to receive instructions. You are going to be given instructions for obtaining information for a project for which you are responsible. Think about what you might want to know and be prepared to ask as many questions as possible. You want detail so keep asking for it. After you have prepared to receive these instructions, select one person to represent the team in the interaction. During receipt of the instructions, your "receiver" can ask for assistance from the group, or the group can intervene and offer assistance if they feel the receiver could use some assistance in obtaining information.

High Context Receivers:

As a team, prepare to receive instructions. You are going to be given instructions for preparing a report to be delivered to a high-status group. You understand the context of both the report and the group to which you will be delivering the report so you don't need a lot of detail. If the presenter gives too many details, interrupt and say you really have all you need. After you have prepared to receive these instructions, select one person to represent the team in the interaction. During receipt of the instructions, your "receiver" can ask for assistance from the group, or the group can intervene and offer assistance if they feel the receiver could use some help.

E-mail Intent vs. Impact

Time Required:

30–45 minutes: 10 minutes to discuss differences in approach, 20 minutes to reframe a series of e-mails, 15 minutes to debrief

Objectives:

To help participants:

1. Identify how e-mail messages can be misinterpreted.
2. Practice identifying alternative potential intentions for e-mail messages.

Materials:

A series of e-mail messages

Process:

1. Briefly discuss the differences between cultural approaches to e-mail messages including:

   • Task vs. Relationship approaches
   • Formal vs. Informal approaches
   • High vs. Low Context

2. Give participants a series of e-mail messages (see Attachment for some suggestions).

Debriefing Questions:

1. How would you respond to this e-mail message?
2. What approach might the sender be using?
3. What could be the positive intention of the sender?
4. How might you respond to this e-mail if you assumed your initial response was correct?
5. How might you respond to this e-mail if the sender had a positive intent?

6. How could you rewrite this e-mail to have a positive impact on you?
7. How might you use this reframing of an e-mail in your daily work?

Debriefing Conclusions:

1. E-mail messages are often misinterpreted because the sender and receiver have different cultural approaches.
2. Reframing the message with a positive intention can allow people to be more effective in accurately perceiving and working with one another.

Optional way to conduct the exercise:

Ask participants to bring an example of an e-mail they have received that they interpreted in a negative manner.

Attachment : Sample E-mail Messages

Miguel: Will arrive at hotel 7 pm. See you then. Donna

My dearest Donna: How is your family? I hope you had a wonderful weekend. I am very excited about our upcoming work together because I always learn so much when we work together. I will arrive at the hotel about 7 pm and hope we can have dinner together and catch up on each other's lives before we begin our project. I spent the weekend hiking with my partner and we saw some beautiful scenery. I have photos that I look forward to sharing with you. I will call you when I get to the hotel. Warmest regards, Miguel.

Sharon: Regarding Q1 results. Off by 10% of target. Clearly not acceptable. Please send your plan for revision.

Harold: Want to discuss my observations of last week's meeting. You are not much of a team player are you? Results are good. Carolyn

Pietre: Want to inform you that due to staff shortages and schedule demands, we have not yet shipped the order that was due to your client in Bogata this week. Efforts being made to ship next week. Emma

Be Specific!

Time Required:

30 minutes: 10 to set up and conduct the exercise, 20 to debrief

Objectives:

To help participants:

1. Experience how often we may assume that others understand what we mean.
2. Identify how important specific language by the speaker can be in creating genuine understanding.
3. Identify how important it can be for the listener to ask questions to ensure effective communication.

Materials:

One sheet of lightweight paper for each team of participants
One sheet for the facilitator

Process:

1. Place participants in teams of two.
2. Explain that the purpose of this exercise is for each team to create a paper "snowflake" that looks exactly like the one you are going to create. Each team will have a "teacher" who will observe your actions and tell the "learner" what to do.
3. Ask each team to sit in chairs that are arranged back to back (so the teacher and learner cannot see each other) and so the teacher in each team can see you. Place chairs so pairs won't be able to hear other pairs, if possible.
4. Make 8–10 manipulations of your sheet of paper, allowing a few seconds after each action to give the teachers time to tell the learners what they want them to do. For example, you might:
    a. Fold the paper in half.
    b. Fold the paper in half again.

    c. Tear off one corner.
    d. Tear off another corner.
    e. Fold the paper again.
    f. Tear out a section of the middle.
    g. Tear out a corner.
    h. Fold the paper one more time.
    i. Tear one more corner.

5. Unfold your piece of paper and invite the learners to do the same and to contrast their "snowflake" with yours.
6. Debrief.

Debriefing Questions:

1. What happened during this exercise?
2. What was most helpful in achieving the goal of replicating the facilitator's snowflake?
3. What was least helpful in achieving the goal of replicating the facilitator's snowflake?
4. What are the implications for cross-cultural communication?

Debriefing Conclusions:

1. When we are not face-to-face (e.g., virtual teams; e-mail) specificity in information provided is useful in creating accurate understanding.
2. Asking for clarification can help create accuracy in understanding.
3. We may not use detail or ask questions if we assume we have a common understanding.

Optional ways to conduct the exercise:

1. This exercise can be conducted in two "rounds." If you use this approach you will need two sheets of paper for each pair and for yourself.
   a. Round 1, the learners are not allowed to talk.
   b. Round 2, the learners are allowed to talk.
2. Instead of folding paper, you can use pens, crayons, or craft material to have "learners" create a picture or an object. This can be great fun with younger participants but also will take a few minutes longer for the exercise.

© Donna Stringer, Ph.D., 2008.

35

My Inner Rules

Time Required:

60 minutes: 10 minutes for lecture, 10 minutes to complete self-assessment, 10 minutes in small group discussion, 30 minutes to debrief

Objectives:

To help participants identify:

1. The inner "rules" each person has learned and how those rules affect our assessment of others.
2. How our assessment of others can affect cross cultural communication.

Materials:

What Are Your Inner Rules? assessment sheets for each participant (see Attachment)

Process:

1. Provide a brief lecture discussing the way each person's demographic characteristics help establish filters that are used to interpret and assess other people's behaviors. Give a few brief examples and ask participants to add their own:
   a. Gender—men and women often interpret the same situation in different ways and are evaluated by those around them based on whether they respond appropriately for their gender culture. When men act "too soft" they may not be seen as masculine; when women act "too tough" they may not be seen as feminine.
   b. Age—differences in response to the same situation based on age. "Gen Y" people may change jobs rapidly based on personal opportunities while "Traditionalists" will often remain in a job out of loyalty to an employer—even when it is not to their personal advantage.

WORKPLACE
NONVERBAL
M–H

c. Race/ethnicity—how cultural biases create different responses to individuals based on how they look or sound. For example, individuals with Asian appearances are often assumed to be immigrants and are treated with surprise when they speak perfect English. African American men are often perceived to be dangerous if they speak with passion.

d. Add your own based on issues relevant to the group you are working with.

2. Add that based on our own personal, cultural, and family backgrounds, our filters develop inner rules that may lead us to define things differently from others we interact with. For example:

a. How we define honesty. Does it mean telling *everything we know*, only *what we think the other person needs to know*, or *only what they ask specifically*?

b. How we work and what we do. Do we assume work is always first or that family is always first? Do we assume we generate our own work assignments or wait to be told what to do by someone with authority?

c. How we approach authority. Do we value equality and therefore are willing to make suggestions and even disagree with the "boss" or do we assume the person with the highest status is responsible for making all decisions?

d. How we communicate. Should we stay calm and "take turns" talking or is it acceptable to overlap and get passionate about a subject?

e. Give your own example based on issues relevant to the group you are working with.

3. Conclude that when people have different filters they often develop different inner rules and misperceive or mislabel others . . . and it is rarely in a positive way. Consequently, it is important to begin by understanding one's own filters and rules to understand why we respond to someone else's behaviors in certain ways.

4. Have individuals complete and score "What Are Your Inner Rules?"

5. Put people in small groups of 4–5 and have them share their inner rules scores looking especially for items in which some of them scored a "0" and others scored a "2." Have them discuss the implications for these differences as they communicate with one another.

6. Debrief.

Debriefing Questions:

1. How did you feel when you were completing the assessment?
2. What insights or thoughts did you have as you were completing the assessment?
3. What happened as you were sharing your scores with others? What observations would you make?
4. What implications did you identify for how inner rules could impact your communication with others?

Debriefing Conclusions:

1. Cultures—which include virtually all of our demographic characteristics—teach us rules that we internalize and that become the filters through which we assess others.
2. When our inner rules are different from the rules of others around us, we often assess them and their behaviors in a negative manner.
3. Becoming more aware of our inner rules can help us avoid negative assessments of others.

Adapted from Theodora Wells. 1980. *Keeping Your Cool Under Fire: Communicating Non-Defensively*. New York: McGraw Hill.

Attachment : What Are Your Inner Rules?

Score the intensity of these rules as they apply to you. 0 = Don't have this rule; 1 = Often feel this urge; 2 = Yep, that's me!

I have to:	I have to:
____ Be in control of the situation	____ Be convincing
____ Be a good team player	____ Do it by myself
____ Be right	____ Appear confident and cool
____ Be loyal	____ Be objective, unemotional
____ Justify myself	____ Be a success
____ Not make waves	____ Be responsible for others
____ Have the answers	____ Do the best I'm capable of
____ Be persistent	____ Take the initiative
____ Break rules to see what happens	____ Follow orders
____ Decide for myself	____ See that things are done right
____ Keep peace at any price	____ Be dependable
____ Make the boss look good	____ Be a nice girl/guy
____ Be the expert	____ Finish it
____ Be logical and rational	____ Go through channels
____ Stick to my principles, ethics	____ Make a track record
____ Stay ahead of the pack	____ Keep this job, not get fired
____ Be above average	____ Prove myself
____ Produce, perform	____ Be consistent
____ Be respected	____ Make myself visible
____ Be perfect	____ Be liked, accepted
____ Improve, develop myself	____ Be in control of myself
____ Conform to what's expected	____ Not question authority
____ Be "In the Know"	____ Be prepared for anything
____ Be on time	____ Be able to take it
____ Come out on top, win	____ Avoid conflict at any cost

Adapted from Theodora Wells. 1980. *Keeping Your Cool Under Fire: Communicating Non-Defensively*. New York: McGraw Hill.

36

Nondefensive Communication

Time Required:

80 minutes: 5 minutes for introduction to cross-cultural issues; 10 minutes to deliver ten tools; 10 minutes for small group preparation; 40 minutes for four role-plays including feedback for each one; 15 minutes to debrief

Objectives:

To help participants:

1. Identify potential cross-cultural exchanges that can create feelings of defensiveness.
2. Identify ten steps that can more effectively manage defensiveness.
3. Practice using nondefensive communication.

Materials:

Handout: Ten steps for Developing Nondefensive Communication (Attachment A)

Case studies (Attachment B)

Process:

1. Provide a brief lecture about some of the cross-cultural issues that can create feelings of defensiveness:
   a. Intentional or unintentional insults or jokes
   b. Intentional or unintentional abuse of status differences
   c. Others as provided by the participants
2. Give a brief lecture regarding the ten steps to nondefensive communication, using Attachment A.
3. Place participants in groups of 3–5; give each group two case studies. Ask each group to select the case study that they would find MOST challenging and prepare to demonstrate the use of some of the ten tools in a role-play of that case study.

4. After 10 minutes, begin the role-plays. Play the "offending" party while the participant selected by each group plays the individual using nondefensive communication. (*Note that you will need to be familiar with all case studies and be prepared to (a) challenge the individual you are role playing with—that is, don't be too easy so the participant has an opportunity to experience the value of the tools, and (b) not be so tough that the participant cannot experience success with the tools.*)

5. After each role-play, ask the entire group to offer feedback about what the participant did well and what might have been done differently.

Debriefing Questions:

1. What feelings/thoughts did you have as we were discussing cross-cultural defensiveness?
2. What challenges came up as you were preparing for the role-play?
3. Which of the ten tools would be easiest for you to use? Why?
4. How can this information be useful to you in your daily life?

Debriefing Conclusions:

1. When statements are made that intentionally or unintentionally relate to personal demographics, we can feel defensive.
2. While a single incident might feel minor to others, it can have deep impact on the target of the comments. Further, if that individual has experienced earlier incidents of the same kind, it can result in defensiveness that feels out of proportion in the moment to others but makes sense in the context of that person's history.
3. When we feel defensive, our communication is often less effective.
4. If we can learn some tools for managing our own reactions, we can not only communicate more effectively, but also create greater understanding and better results.

Optional ways to conduct the exercise:

1. Ask participants to identify their own case studies based on some interaction they have had across cultural differences (e.g., age, gender, status, ethnicity, nationality, religion, etc.) and create a role-play in their small groups to present to the entire class.

2. Ask participants to share situations in which they have felt defensive and discuss those within small groups, looking for which of the ten tools they might have found most useful. Small groups can then report common themes to the larger group without any role-plays occurring.

Developed by Donna Stringer, Ph.D., 2008. Based on Theodora Wells. (1980). *Keeping Your Cool Under Fire: Communicating Non-Defensively*. New York: McGraw-Hill.

Attachment A: Ten Steps for Developing Nondefensive Communication

1. Buy time.
    a. To gain space to think.
    b. To find a way to say "no."
    c. To get your feelings under control.
    For example, "I will need to think about that"; "Let me get back to you."
2. Respond only to the "positive surface content"
    For example, someone says it is good to see you because you haven't been around lately (suggesting you have not been working).
    You could say: "Thanks, it is nice to be here—working in the field has been productive but I have missed seeing people in the office."
3. If surface meaning is negative, question the assumptions.
    For example, someone accuses you of being angry.
    You could say: "What makes you think I am angry?"
4. Name the "game."
    For example, someone continually puts down your suggestions.
    You could say: "It feels like we are competing for whose ideas are best and I would rather not do that."
5. Give and ask for feedback.
6. Make the implicit explicit
    For example, someone tells you, an Asian American, that you speak very good English.
    You say: "Why would you think I couldn't speak English? I was born in the United States and English is the only language I know."
7. Report (don't express) the feelings.
    For example, "I am feeling a bit defensive so I need some time to think about what we are doing."
8. Check your reality—find someone you trust whom you can share your experience and feelings with. Use this to test your perceptions and potential alternative explanations.
9. Practice nonresponsiveness—listen but do not respond.
10. Use a close-off statement or Action.
    For example, someone continues talking about an issue that you feel defensive about but is saying nothing new—simply repeating the same information over and over.
    You could say: "I believe we have said everything that needs to be said."

Developed by Donna Stringer, Ph.D., 2008. Based on Theodora Wells. (1980). *Keeping Your Cool Under Fire: Communicating Non-Defensively*. New York: McGraw-Hill.

Attachment B: Case Studies

1. You have become very involved in a new employee network. You are passionate about the issues the network is working on and have donated a lot of time to their work because you feel it will be a great benefit to the organization as well as to the network members. You have been very careful, however, not to let it interfere with meeting all of your work assignments in a timely, quality manner. Your manager, however, has not felt very supportive and at today's staff meeting he made a snide remark that "I would assign you to the new project but you don't have any time left now that you are working full-time for the network."

2. You have recently been appointed to a management position and have heard many "joking" comments that if you weren't (black, female, young, etc.—fill in a demographic characteristic that works for you), you would never have been promoted. You have tried to assume that those making the comments were really teasing but it has happened often enough that it is beginning to get under your skin. You are in the hallway with two of your subordinates when a client enters the conversation and one of the employees introduces you as "the new (black, female, etc.) manager, as if your demographic characteristic is all that defines you.

3. You have recently hired a young Asian female right out of school. She is an outstanding performer and you are very proud of her. One of your peers asks you, "What in the world were you thinking, hiring someone with a tattoo? Our clients will never work with her."

4. You are a female whose performance has always been stellar. Your new manager continues to comment about being surprised at how many women there are in the company who have never been promoted. He frequently says it must be that the women have not performed at a high enough level for promotion because "with the focus on female talent lately, if someone was even mediocre, she would have been promoted."

5. You have a slight accent (either because you are from a different region of the country or because you are an immigrant). You are discussing a new project with your work team and someone says they don't think you should be in charge of it because it will be a "virtual" team and others cannot understand your accent on the telephone. You have been teased about your accent before but have never been accused of not being understandable—or of having it affect your job assignments.

6. Your work team is discussing what to do as a holiday celebration when one of your peers turns to you and says, "Hey, are you going to be insulted if we do a Christmas party? Aren't you (Moslem/Jewish/Atheist) or something?"

7. You are one of few women on your work team. The manager is planning a team building event and has decided to take everyone to a remote location where they can hike and fish. You don't object to either hiking or fishing but do feel that the remote location is not necessarily safe—or something you would enjoy participating in. You love the idea of a team building event and are concerned that the manager has made the decisions without team involvement, which feels contradictory to the purpose for the meeting.

8. You are standing outside of your manager's office waiting to meet with her when you hear a colleague telling a joke that was rather derogatory to a group in which you belong. You hope your manager will let your colleague know that the joke is inappropriate and offensive, but instead she laughs. You feel a mixture of disappointment and resentment at your manager's reaction. It is not the first time that you had heard such derogatory remarks being made without them being challenged.

Developed by Donna Stringer, Ph.D., 2008. Based on Theodora Wells. (1980). *Keeping Your Cool Under Fire: Communicating Non-Defensively.* New York: McGraw-Hill.

37

My Name Is . . .

Time Required:

60 minutes: 10 minutes for original lecture, 30 minutes for two small group conversations, 20 minutes for debrief

Objectives:

To help participants identify:

1. The importance of names as part of personal identity.
2. Different cultural ways of naming people.
3. The importance of calling people by the name they prefer—and pronouncing it properly.

Materials:

None

Process:

1. Lecture regarding cultural and historical issues around names, allowing participants to add any information they have about how people are named. In each instance ask participants what the "rule" tells them about cultural values:
   a. In some cultures a person's family name comes first and their given name comes last; in other cultures it is the reverse. (*Note that this is a clue to whether the culture values individualism or group orientation.*)
   b. In the United States, African slaves were routinely stripped of their African names and given the names of the family that "owned" them.
   c. In the United States, many immigrants are given "new," easier-to-pronounce, names by immigration or school personnel.
   d. In some cultures, one's given name carries significance, representing the family's hope for the child, or signifying some characteristic of the individual.

e. In some cultures (e.g., Ghana and Bali) the name indicates a child's gender, birth order, or day of the week he or she was born. In other cultures (e.g., Ireland) a family name will tell you the family's geographic and religious history. In still others (Middle Eastern and African countries) a name identifies the family, ethnic group, and/or tribal affiliation.

f. In some cultures women take their husband's family name upon marriage.

2. Place people in groups of 3–5 and give them 15 minutes for the following discussion:

a. What are the origins of your name—both given name and family name? What would your name tell me about you?

b. How do you feel about your name? Why?

c. Has your name ever changed? Who made the change? Why?

d. What impact did your name change have on you?

3. In the larger group ask what observations or insights they would make based on the short discussion they just had in the small groups.

4. Keeping people in the same small groups, allow them to continue their discussion, answering the following questions.

a. Have you ever been called a name you didn't like? By whom? Why? What impact did it have on you?

b. If your employer insisted that you change your name to one commonly held by the other gender in order to keep your job, how might that feel? What might you do?

c. How could you handle names of those you interact with every day in order to create an environment that feels respectful to everyone with whom you come in contact?

Debriefing Questions:

1. What observations would you make about names based on the information we have looked at and your small group discussion?

2. What feelings did these discussions evoke for you?

3. Did anything surprise you? What? Why?

4. What were the ideas for creating a respectful environment?

Debriefing Conclusions:

1. Names are more important in some cultures than in others—and for some individuals than for others.

2. Cultures assign the meaning of names and every individual gains some portion of their self-identity from their name based on that cultural assignment.

3. Allowing others to make choices about what to be called—and how to be addressed—is one factor in being perceived as respectful in your communication.
4. Specific tips for managing names include:
    a. Learn to pronounce a person's name correctly.
    b. Ask how people are addressed in their own language and when you should use a formal address, family name, or given names.
    c. Ask people about their names—how they got them and how to pronounce them (and do not assume based on how someone looks that they are not U.S. born).
    d. If a name has been "assigned" to make it easier for others to pronounce, asking about someone's "original" name and learning how to pronounce it may lead to a deeper conversation, and the ability to show greater respect by calling someone by the name they prefer.
    e. Do not assign other people nicknames. If they have a nickname and enjoy using it, they will likely tell you as trust builds.
    f. Do not use slang terms (for example, *honey, dearie, bud,* and so on.)

Optional ways to conduct the exercise:

If you are working with a group that you have ongoing contact with, consider "assigning" each person a new name and requiring that they use it for several hours or days before you conduct this exercise. Doing this allows the conversation to go much deeper concerning how names impact identity and how strongly we can feel if someone else changes our names. In assigning names, change the person's identity as much as possible: give men names that are commonly used for women, and vice versa. Give people names identified with other ethnic or religious groups, and so on.

38

PALS Dialogue

Time Required:

100 minutes: 20 minutes for lecture, 10 minutes to introduce the PALS tool, 10 minutes to prepare for a dialogue, 30 minutes for the dialogue, 30 minutes to debrief

WORKPLACE
EDUCATION
VERBAL
M–H

Objectives:

To help participants:

1. Learn how dialogue can improve communication, especially around subjects that are challenging or difficult.
2. Learn a tool for preparing for dialogues.
3. Experience using the dialogue tools, PALS, in conducting a dialogue.

Materials:

Lecture on Dialogue (Attachment A)

PALS planning tool for each participant (Attachment B)

A dialogue topic selected by the facilitator to reflect a current controversial issue in the news media or specific to the organization in which the training is occurring

Process:

1. Give a brief lecture about dialogue—see Attachment A.
2. Give an introduction to the PALS planning tool—see Attachment B.
3. Give participants the issue you will be asking them to have a dialogue about and allow them 5–10 minutes to prepare individually for the dialogue using the PALS tool.
4. Place participants in small groups and allow them 30 minutes to conduct a dialogue.
5. Debrief.

Debriefing Questions:

1. What were your feelings/thoughts/insights as you used PALS to prepare for the dialogue?
2. What were your feelings/thoughts/insights as you participated in the dialogue?
3. What did you learn from the conversation?
4. How can this process be used to improve cross-cultural communication in your organization?
5. How can you, personally, use this process?

Debriefing Conclusions:

1. Conducting a dialogue can allow for a deeper level of understanding of another person and their experiences and perspectives.
2. Having a deeper level of understanding can improve both cross-cultural relationships as well as decision-making processes.
3. The more preparation for a cross-cultural conversation, the less likely it is to result in misunderstanding.

Attachment A: Lecture On Dialogue

Deliver information about Dialogue using the following outline and information.

Dialogue is useful . . . :

- When you want to build trust.
- When you want to learn more about another person's point of view.
- When you want to gain a deeper level of understanding to facilitate a stronger relationship or enhanced communication and/or problem solving.

State that sometimes people are unclear as to when to have a dialogue. It is really anytime that you want to learn more about another person's point of view. It can occur at lunch, during the work day, or any other time that a good opportunity presents itself.

Dialogue:

- Is a conversation with a center but no sides.
- Allows us to think beyond limits.
- May dissolve—but not solve—problems (if you identify through listening that you actually do not have a difference of opinion).
- Requires suspension of status and judgments.
- Has a single focus: greater understanding.

Make the following points:
- Dialogue is not a debate.
- It is not about right or wrong.
- It is an ideal way to learn more about another person.
- It is a method for gaining understanding about someone else's experiences that you might not share—for gaining cross-cultural understanding.
- It is not a problem-solving session. Problem solving can be more successfully done once a meaningful dialogue has taken place and greater understanding has been gained.

Dialogue is helped by:

- Courage to share your ideas/perspectives.
- Authenticity.
- Listening to self and others.
- Allowing silence without interruption.
- Focus/being present.
- Taking responsibility.

POTENTIAL EXPANSION POINTS:

- Dialogue must be real: This is not about being politically correct. If you use it that way, you will be neither genuine nor learn about someone else. Unreal conversations take personal energy and reduce trust and effectiveness.

- Listening to yourself is critical. When you get that "gut" feeling that something isn't right—listen to it and learn from it.
- Being focused/present: In a fast-paced results-oriented performance culture, if you cannot be present to another person you will not learn about them. they will not trust you. While multi-tasking may have gotten you where you are today, you cannot multitask during a dialogue.
- Dialogue requires taking responsibility for your own listening and sharing.

Dialogue is hindered by . . . :

- Minimizing differences—focusing on similarities.
- Blind spots—not knowing what we don't know.
- Performance culture/drive for results.
- Fear
  - Of making things worse.
  - Of loss of friendship and/or conflict.
  - Of negative career impact.
  - Of challenging our own belief system.

POTENTIAL EXPANSION POINTS:

- Avoid the temptation to "go for the safe place" and look for where you agree. There is little to learn from someone with whom you agree. Look for the places you disagree and identify how those differences might benefit each of you. You can end with similarities but don't start there.
- Truly believing that there is something about another person's experience you don't know can lead to interesting questions—both for the purpose of getting to know that person better and for expanding your own information base. People of color, women, lesbians and gays, as well as other "cultural outsider" groups often report that when they share a difficult experience they have had, the listener immediately discounts it or disbelieves it. Use dialogue to "step into another person's world, with belief."
- In a fast-paced culture, in which productivity or task is often a primary focus, a conversation that seemingly does not have a specific, tangible outcome may not be viewed as a good use of time. When people realize that investing time in gaining deeper understanding smoothes the way to more successful problem solving in the long term, dialogue will become easier.
- And, of course, that monster *fear*! We often avoid discussing challenging issues because we are afraid. And afraid with good intent. We don't want to make things worse, lose friends, have arguments, lose our job, or challenge our own self-image in a negative way. That is why we use the PALS tool to prepare.
- Good dialogue often begins by acknowledging which of these things has stopped us from having good conversations before. Think about this before getting started. What has stopped you personally from being as genuine as possible and from having conversations that could allow you to share yourself with others and learn about them? Because without these discussions we will not learn about cross-cultural differences or develop effective cross-cultural communication and understanding.

The Tool:

The PALS tool helps us overcome the barriers and prepare for success. We begin with planning. We ask about the other person's perspective, listening fully, and then we share our own perspective. The left-hand column lists the four steps to dialogue. The right-hand column lists *some things you might do* in each step. You will not always do every item in the right-hand column, and you may add additional things. And you may not do the last three steps in the order listed (*facilitator see note below*). The important thing is to ensure that each step gets covered. (Give some *brief, relevant examples*... you may not go through each bullet, but pick one or two key bullets from each of the four areas.)

> *Note to facilitators: There is often a concern on the part of people who have been marginalized in a culture when they are asked to share information about themselves or their experiences and perspective—especially if they have had any experience of personal information sharing having a negative result. Sharing our personal experiences, thoughts, and perspectives can make us vulnerable and if I am in a marginalized group I may already feel vulnerable. For this reason, it is often appropriate and culturally effective for the person with the highest level of status or who belongs to an "insider" group to tell about themselves before asking about the other. Consider this issue when deciding whether to ask first or share first.*

Attachment B: Preparing with PALS

P-repare	• Identify your own preferences for communication styles. • Identify your interest/curiosity—why do you want a dialogue? • Identify your fears—challenge their reality. • Identify what you know (or think you know) and what you want to know about the other. • Identify and prepare to share your intent.
A-sk	• How can we understand one another better? (use behavior based words) • How can we be more effective with each other? • How is your experience similar to/different from mine?
L-isten	• Listen to understand—don't miss an experience that is not yours or that is unbelievable to you. • Learn through empathy. • Listen to the words, the feelings, and the nonverbals. • Listen without interruption; paraphrase for accuracy. • Look for style similarities and differences.
S-hare	• Share your experiences, perspectives, values, and feelings. • Speak for yourself, not a group, and don't ask anyone else to speak for their group. • Solicit feedback about how you impact others and ways to increase your effectiveness. • Seek multiple perspectives; think "and," not "or." • Share feedback in specific, behavioral terms when asked.

39

If I Woke up Tomorrow . . .

Time Required:

105 minutes: 5 minutes to set up, 20 minutes for first segregated conversation, 15 minutes to share first discussion, 20 minutes for second segregated conversation, 15 minutes to share second discussion, 20 minutes to debrief, 10 minutes to share ideas for more effective communication and closure

Objectives:

To help participants:

1. Identify perceptions across group differences.
2. Share perceptions across groups.
3. Have dialogues that allow for more accurate perceptions.
4. Identify more effective ways of communicating across group differences.

Materials:

Two easels with paper pads

Multiple marking pens

Two rooms

Process:

1. Explain the purpose for the exercise and the entire process they will experience (*Note: It will be important for some people to know that while they are being segregated, they will ultimately be back in an integrated group*).
2. Ask people to complete the "If I Woke Up Tomorrow" attachment individually.
3. Segregate the class into groups based on the group differences being examined (e.g., gender, ethnicity, occupation, etc.). Ask each group to share and discuss their individual responses, listing on an easel the commonly held perceptions of the other group. Note that there will be differences among

the individual members of each group so you are asking them to list those perceptions that are most common, although not necessarily unanimous. Ask each group to also list 1–3 questions they "have always wanted to ask the other group."

4. Return to the large group asking each small group to report its perceptions and its questions. At this stage, each group is to simply report its results and the other group is simply to listen. Questions of clarification can be asked, but discussion does not take place.

5. Segregate the groups again. This time each group is to take the other group's perceptions and questions and prepare a response to them. Which perceptions are accurate, somewhat accurate, and not at all accurate? How would the group respond to the other group's questions about themselves? Again, you are not looking for a unanimous response but for the most common response, along with information about the differences within the group.

6. Return to the large group with each small group sharing its responses to the other group's perceptions about them and the answers to the other group's questions about them.

7. Debrief the experience.

8. Chart the ideas for cross-group communication and summarize them before adjourning.

Debriefing Questions:

1. How did you feel when I first told you I was going to segregate you by group? Why?

2. What was the most challenging part of this exercise? Why?

3. How did you feel having the conversation within your own group?

4. How did you feel when sharing your group's perception with the other group?

5. How did you feel while listening to the other group share its perceptions about your group?

6. What observations would you make about what you have experienced or heard today?

7. What ONE idea would you share to improve communication across these groups?

Debriefing Conclusions:

1. Cross-group perceptions are often based on cultural stereotypes.

2. Cultural stereotypes may have some element of truth and may also be wrong.

3. Cultural stereotypes may be generally true for each group but wrong for individuals within each group.
4. When we examine our own perceptions and share them with the other person(s), we are more likely to have accurate information.

Optional ways to conduct the exercise:

This exercise is particularly useful for conversations about perceptions and improved relationships across gender, race/ethnicity, age, or occupational categories. Depending on the group differences being explored, the language and questions used in the handout will change.

Adapted with permission from *Bridging the Gender Gap* (1995) by Louise Yolton Eberhardt, Whole Person Associates, Inc., Duluth, Minnesota.

Attachment: If I Woke up Tomorrow . . .

Instructions: Consider that you wake up tomorrow morning a member of the other gender. In what ways would your work life change in the following areas? Jot down a few words in each area below that describe the changes you think would occur.

1. Topics of conversations:

2. Relationships with others (who?):

3. Social events:

4. Occcupational options:

5. Salary/benefits:

6. Education/training/development opportunities:

7. Perceptions others have of me:

8. How I interact with my community:

9. Other:

Adapted with permission from *Bridging the Gender Gap* (1995) by Louise Yolton Eberhardt, Whole Person Associates, Inc., Duluth, Minnesota.

40

Building Style Proficiency

Time Required:

60 minutes: 20 minutes lecture, 5 minutes individual profile, 20 minutes style shifting exercise, 15 minutes debrief

Objectives:

To help participants:

1. Learn a range of communication styles that can impact perception and communication effectiveness.
2. Examine how different styles can lead to misperception, potential conflict, or negative communication impacts.
3. Identify one's personal communication style preferences.
4. Identify the team's communication style profile.
5. Identify how to use the team profile for maximum communication effectiveness.

Materials:

Communication Styles Continuum PowerPoint slide (Attachment A)

Communication Styles Continua Described Handout with definitions for each participant (Attachment B)

Communication Styles Contrast Worksheet for each participant (Attachment A) printed

Process:

1. Using the Communication Styles PowerPoint slide and Communication Styles Described handout, briefly describe each style contrast, asking participants to identify how the style at one end of the continuum is likely to be perceived by the style at the other end of the continuum. Make the point, through their own examples, that each end of each style continuum can, with the best of intentions, be misperceived by someone using a different style.

2. Using the Communication Styles Worksheet, ask each individual to identify their preferred style by placing an X on *each* line where their preferred style is. Make the point that while most people shift styles based on context, you are asking individuals to identify where they are *most* comfortable on each continuum—not where they adapt to based on context. After they have placed their six X's on the page, they should "connect the X's" so they have a visual picture of their style profile. Ask individuals to identify the ONE style they have the greatest difficulty with when someone else is using it.

3. Place people in triads. Each person will take turns telling their practice partners which style they find most challenging and, using the tips for effectiveness at the bottom of each definition page, practice using their most challenging style in talking to their practice partners. If people have difficulty thinking about what to talk about, ask them to tell their partners what they have learned about communication styles and how they intend to share the information with their work team or family.

Debriefing Questions:

1. What did you learn from this experience?
2. How did it feel to use your least preferred style?
3. How can you use this information to be more effective at work and at home?

Debriefing Conclusions:

1. All styles are effective based on context.
2. We tend to see in negative terms those using styles that we don't prefer.
3. We can learn to use our least preferred styles if we practice doing so.
4. When we learn to use other styles, it often changes the way we see those who are using those styles most naturally/regularly.

Exercise developed by Donna Stringer, Ph.D., 2007; Communication styles continua originally developed by Dr. Janet Bennett and Dr. Milton Bennett, 1993.

Attachment A: Communication Styles

Linear	Circular
Direct	Indirect
Low Context	High Context
Attached	Detached
Idea-Focused	Person-Focused
Task-Focused	Relationship-Focused

Exercise developed by Donna Stringer, Ph.D., 2007; Communication styles continua originally developed by Dr. Janet Bennett and Dr. Milton Bennett, 1993.

Attachment B: Communication Styles Continua Described—Handout

LINEAR	CIRCULAR
Communication is conducted in a straight line, moving in a linear way toward the main point. "Getting to the point" is very important and the point is stated explicitly. Not getting to the point quickly is seen as a time waster.	Communication is conducted in a circular manner around the main point. The point may be left unstated because the verbal and nonverbal information provided is sufficient for understanding. Stating the point explicitly is seen as insulting to the other person.
To be effective with this style: • Be brief. • Preface your remarks with "the pint is . . ." • Provide only as much explanation as the other person needs. • Be explicit about the main point. • Do not deviate from the main point.	**To be effective with this style:** • Be elegant and flowing with your remarks. • Never preface a comment with "the point is . . ." • Embellish your remarks with stories and anecdotes. Let the story make the point. • Let the other person infer the meaning of your comments from the story.
DIRECT	**INDIRECT**
What one means is stated in a very straightforward and direct manner. There is no "beating around the bush." Directness is equated with honesty and respect for the other person.	Meaning is conveyed by subtle means such as nonverbal behavior, parables and stories, suggestions and implication. Indirectness is equated with politeness and respect for the other person.
To be effective with this style: • Respect the other person's time. • Don't create ambiguity or uncertainty by avoiding the issue. • Be straightforward.	**To be effective with this style:** • Respect the other person's feelings. • Don't put the other person on the spot by being too direct. • Be polite.
LOW CONTEXT	**HIGH CONTEXT**
The context of the communication is not assumed to be known. Things must be explained clearly and unambiguously. Meaning must be expressed precisely.	The context for communication is assumed to be known. Hence, it is unnecessary, even insulting to explain things and state meaning precisely. Meaning is taken from context.
To be effective with this style: • Always communicate clearly, completely, and unambiguously. • Don't leave understanding to chance.	**To be effective with this style:** • Always respect the other person's understanding of the situation. • Leave understanding up to the other person.

ATTACHED (EMOTIONAL)	DETACHED (UNEMOTIONAL)
Communication is carried out with feeling and emotion. Issues are discussed with passion and commitment. Communication is very expressive. Sharing one's values and feelings about the issues is highly valued. **To be effective with this style:** • State your views with passion and conviction. • If you care about an idea, show it. • Bring yourself as a person into the discussion and show who you are.	Communication is carried out in a calm and impersonal manner. This is equated with objectivity, which is valued. Highly expressive, emotional, and engaged communication is inappropriate because this is seen as personalizing the issues and as biased. **To be effective with this style:** • State your views dispassionately. • Avoid being overly emotional. • Avoid personalizing the discussion—keep yourself out of it.
IDEA-FOCUSED	**PERSON-FOCUSED**
The emphasis is on ideas that are seen as separate from the person. Thus, disagreement with another person's ideas is acceptable and even valued. It is not seen as a personal attack. **To be effective with this style:** • Listen carefully to the ideas being discussed. • If you disagree with someone's idea, say so. • Because a person's ideas are wrong doesn't mean there is something wrong with the person.	The emphasis is on the person, hence great importance is attached to the feelings of the other person. Issues and ideas *are not* separated from the person. Thus, disagreement with someone's ideas must be handled very carefully. **To be effective with this style:** • Respond to the person. Be attentive to feelings. • In your communication, be careful not to hurt the other person's feelings. • Understand that an attack on someone's idea is an attack on that person.
TASK-FOCUSED	**RELATIONSHIP-FOCUSED**
Communication focuses on the task at hand and getting it done. The other person's feelings are secondary. Group harmony is secondary to task completion. **To be effective with this style:** • Keep focusing on the task at hand. • Don't allow too much small talk to sidetrack the task. • Clarify the task. • Publicly sanction slackards.	Communication is focused on relationships. Maintaining group harmony is central. The task is secondary. Task completion must not come at the expense of the group or person. **To be effective with this style:** • Make certain that your concern with the task doesn't come at the expense of someone's feelings and the well-being of the group. • Praise the participants for their good work. • Never publicly call down a colleague.

Exercise developed by Donna Stringer, Ph.D., 2007; Communication styles continua originally developed by Dr. Janet Bennett and Dr. Milton Bennett, 1993.

41

Build a Structure

Time Required:

45 minutes: 10 minutes set-up, 20 minutes activity, and 15 minutes debrief

Objectives:

To help participants:

1. Experience diverse team building.
2. Practice communication skills in an ambiguous environment.
3. Practice leadership skills in a diverse group.
4. Accomplish a task with a diverse group.
5. Achieve synergy in group diversity for creative problem solving.

Materials:

Long tables or grouped desks where teams of 4–5 can work

Colored construction paper

Scotch tape and glue sticks

Colored markers

Scissors

Small prizes (candy and pens work well)

Process:

1. Divide the group into diverse teams of 4–5 participants (mix gender, ethnicity, race, age, etc.).
2. Give each team one minute to select a leader by any means they choose.
3. Ask team leaders to collect group "supplies" (2 pairs of scissors, 15–20 sheets of construction paper, 2 Scotch tapes, 2 glue sticks, 2 markers).
4. Explain that the task is to design and build "a structure" using the materials. "Structure" is to be defined by the group. Role of the leader is also defined by the group.

5. Set the ground rules:
   No talking or writing during the exercise.
   Drawing and gesturing are permitted.
   The period of silence begins immediately.
   Teams have 20 minutes to complete the exercise.
6. During the exercise, observe the teams to ensure they are not "cheating" by talking or writing. Note any interesting dynamics that occur during the exercise.
7. Signal remaining time by writing on the board 10 minutes, 5 minutes, and 1 minute remaining.
8. Allow the group to talk at the end of the exercise. Ask the team leader to describe the "structure" for the entire group. Identify the "winning" team (optional). (The most "creative" structure receives a prize. You may arbitrarily select the winner or allow the teams to vote. Consolation prizes may be given.)

Debriefing Questions:

1. How was the leader chosen in your group? What was the role of the leader, if any, during the exercise? What role did culture play in (a) how the leader was chosen and/or (b) the role of the leader?
2. How did the group reach a decision on "structure design"? How was the design communicated to the group?
3. How did the group communicate during the building process? What were some of the obstacles and advantages in using nonverbal communication? What role did culture play in this?
4. How did the group assign roles and tasks? Did people fall naturally into certain tasks or was there confusion? What role did culture play in this?
5. Did diversity contribute to a more creative project? Why or why not?
6. How does this exercise reflect real-life circumstances for individuals? In organizations? How is it different?

Debriefing Conclusions:

1. Diversity among team members may enhance creative solutions to problems.
2. Leadership in diverse settings is usually affected by cultural definitions of leadership—and can lead to misperceptions or conflict if there are different cultural perspectives represented in the group.
3. Nonverbal communication is impacted by culture and if there are cultural differences in a group they can hinder or enhance understanding.

4. Creative processes are culturally defined and can produce a wide range of products.
5. Teams developing an effective means for communication/collaboration across cultural differences have a wider range of possible solutions.

Optional way to conduct the exercise:

This exercise can be used as an icebreaker. Facilitators can emphasize different aspects of the exercise, depending on their interests and the theme of the class/presentation.

This exercise makes a nice segue into lectures/presentations on team building, leadership styles, or communication styles. Creativity stems from team collaboration: Structures have ranged from space stations to temples to shopping centers. Participants have even used their own bodies as parts of the structure and decorated themselves.

Adapted from an exercise by Marcella Simon, Hemispheres Learning.

42

Talking Through Touch

Time Required:

45 minutes: 10 minutes for lecture and discussion, 5 minutes to complete assessment, 15 minutes in small group discussion, 15 minutes to debrief

Objectives:

To help participants identify:

1. Different cultural meanings about touching.
2. Individual preferences regarding touch—and where those preferences originated.
3. When touch is a form of culturally appropriate communication.

Materials:

One copy for each participant of the Touch Assessment (Attachment)

Process:

1. Give a brief lecture regarding culture and touch:
   a. Physical touch in business relationships is positive in some cultures (designating trust and relationship) but negative in others (designating power differences or dominance).
   b. In cultures in which touch is used to underscore power, it is the more powerful person who has the "right" to touch the less powerful person first.
   c. Greetings in most cultures involve some form of touch but that form can vary considerably from handshakes to hugs and/or kisses.
   d. In some cultures touch that is appropriate for one gender may not be appropriate for the other gender.
2. Invite participants to discuss the various forms of touch they have encountered in work environments, what meaning they communicated, and how they came to understand the intended meaning.
3. Have participants complete the Touch Assessment.
4. In small groups of 3–5 have participants share their answers to the assessment. Ask them to identify implications of the

similarities and differences among them if they were a work team.

5. Debrief in the large group.

Debriefing Questions:

1. How did you feel as you were completing the assessment? Did you have any "a-ha moments"? What were they?
2. What observations would you make about the communication of touch from this discussion?
3. What implications did you identify from your similarities or differences?
4. How can you use this information to use touch as a communication tool in a culturally appropriate manner?

Debriefing Conclusions:

1. There are both cultural and personal preferences for use of touch in interpersonal relations, especially in a business (educational) setting.
2. Different preferences for touch can lead to misperception and negative communication impact.
3. Telling others if touch is personally uncomfortable for you—even when it is the cultural norm—is important to retaining one's own comfort and reducing interpersonal stress that could have unintended negative consequences for relationships.
4. Learning to expand one's preferences to behave in a culturally effective manner in new settings will increase one's cultural competency.

Note to Facilitators:

In the United States, Canada, and some other northern European countries, touch is modified, if not controlled, by laws related to sexual harassment in the workplace. This is not an exercise intended to result in a discussion about legal issues. If you are using this exercise, be sure you know what the law is related to sexual harassment.

More important, know that a huge percentage of women (up to 50 percent), and a large percentage of men (up to 35 percent), have experienced some form of physical or sexual abuse during their lifetimes. This exercise could also raise those issues when you begin asking people why they are uncomfortable with some forms of touch. If you experience ANY resistance to this discussion, do not push people to participate. It could result in surfacing feelings and issues that are far beyond the scope of this exercise—and beyond the skills of most facilitators.

Attachment: Touch Assessment

1. What type of touch is comfortable for me in a business setting?
2. What type of touch is uncomfortable for me in a business setting?
   a. Why?
   b. Where did I learn this comfort or discomfort?
3. From whom is touch comfortable for me in a business setting?
   a. Why?
4. From whom is touch uncomfortable for me in a business setting?
   a. Why?
5. Who am I comfortable touching in a business setting?
   a. Why?
6. When I touch someone else in a business setting, what are the messages I am attempting to communicate?
7. What strategies might I use to identify what messages others are perceiving when I touch them?
8. What strategies might I use to communicate to others when I am uncomfortable with touch I receive?

43

He Learned She Learned

Time Required:

45 minutes: 20 minutes for activity, 25 minutes debrief

Objectives:

To help participants:

1. Identify learned gender expectations.
2. Discuss individual differences within gender groups.
3. Explore the impact of gender expectations on cross-gender communication.

WORKPLACE
HIGHER
EDUCATION
VERBAL
NONVERBAL
L–M

Materials:

Chart paper

Markers

Process:

1. Divide participants by gender (groups of 10–12).
2. Ask each group to develop two lists on chart paper:
   a. 10 Commandments I Learned That My Gender Must Do
   b. 10 Commandments I Learned That My Gender Must Not Do
3. Tell groups to build consensus, allowing for individual differences. They are not seeking 100 percent agreement.

Debriefing Questions:

1. Where do messages about gender expectations originate?
2. What differences/similarities did you notice within the same-gender groups? What was the source of those differences (e.g., generation, nationality, etc.)? How were differences resolved?
3. How do these messages influence the way we view those who don't "abide by the rules"?

4. How do these messages influence the way we communicate with one another? How is communication affected if someone "acts right" or "doesn't act right"?

Debriefing Conclusions:

1. Messages about gender expectations are received early in life.
2. Gender messages influence our perception of self/others.
3. Perception about gender may differ within a group based on age, nationality, or other cultural influences.
4. Gender assumptions affect the way we communicate and treat one another.
5. Awareness of our gender expectations can help us improve respectful business communications with both men and women

44

I Think—You Feel

Time Required:

65 minutes: 10 minutes for introduction, 15 minutes for preparation, 20 minutes for four presentations; 20 minutes for two debriefs

Objectives:

To help participants:

1. Understand personal preferences for the use of thinking or feeling language in communication.
2. Explore how thinking or feeling language can impact a presentation.
3. Design a presentation focused on either thinking or feeling language.
4. Identify how a presentation can be designed to effectively communicate with audience members who prefer both feeling and thinking language.

Materials:

Presentation Style Preferences Handout (Attachment A)
Index cards with sample presentation topics (Attachment B)
Chart paper
Color markers

Process:

1. Present an introduction regarding the difference in Thinking and Feeling language using Attachment A.
2. Divide participants into four teams of 4–5 and give two teams (Teams A and B) one topic and two teams (Teams C and D) a second topic.
3. Give each team 15 minutes to prepare a presentation on their topic and select a member to make the presentation.
   Teams A and C develop a 5 minute "thinking" presentation
   Teams B and D develop a 5 minute "feeling" presentation

4. One set (Team A and Team B) presents to the whole group (5 minutes each).
5. Debrief with the whole group (10 minutes).
6. Repeat presentations and debriefing with Teams C and D.

Debriefing Questions:

1. How comfortable were you with the assignment? Were you a thinking/feeling team?
2. What were some of the challenges in designing your presentation? How did you resolve these?
3. When the final products were presented, what were the strengths/weaknesses of the thinking/feeling language?
4. How easy/difficult would it be to combine your thinking and feeling presentations into one presentation? Challenges?

Debriefing Conclusions:

1. Individuals have a preference for receiving and delivering information with either thinking or feeling language.
2. Personal communication preferences influence presentation design.
3. Effective presentation design allows for a combination of styles.

Optional ways to conduct the exercise:

Give teams A and B and Teams C and D time after their initial presentations to work together to create a combined presentation that includes both thinking and feeling language. This option will add an additional 40 minutes: 15 minutes to prepare, 10 minutes for two presentations, 15 minutes to debrief.

© Patricia Cassiday, Ed.D. and Donna Stringer, Ph.D., 2008.

Attachment A: Presentation Style Preferences Handout

Our personal communication style influences the way we prefer to receive information. Personal preferences also impact our delivery of information to others. Effective presentation design requires consideration of our personal preferences and the preferences of others. The following tips can be useful when communicating information to a diverse audience.

Tips for "Feeling" presentations:

- Use pictures, graphics, color
- Use stories, metaphors (circular approach)
- Stress harmony, group contributions, feelings
- Seek consensus, group feedback

Tips for "Thinking" presentations:

- Use charts, data, numbers
- Use bullets to make points
- Use clear, direct language (linear approach)
- Emphasize expertise/authority of the presenter
- Develop an "action plan" or summary of information at the end

Attachment B: Sample Presentation Topics

You recently learned that you will be merging with another organization. You are presenting the strategic plan for the merger.

Due to a decline in enrollment, 25 percent of the schools in your district must be closed. You are presenting the plan to the school board, outlining a plan for deciding which schools will be closing.

Your organization is conducting a global immunization program. You are experiencing passive resistance from women in third-world countries. Your presentation is for the United Nations on how you hope to overcome this resistance.

Your city has just received federal funds for improving transportation. There is a perceived inequity between high-speed trains, surface busses, and roads for privately owned vehicles. Your presentation is a proposal to the transportation committee of the city council describing how to deal with the perceived inequity.

You designate a current topic relevant to your organization.

45

What a Funny Thing to Say!

**WORKPLACE
EDUCATION
NONVERBAL
L**

Time Required:

30 minutes: 10 minute for exercise, 20 minutes for debrief

Objectives:

To help participants:

1. Practice identifying messages and values in cross-cultural sayings and proverbs.
2. Identify the cross-cultural implications of using and hearing sayings and proverbs.

Materials:

Attachment: Cross-Cultural Sayings and Proverbs

Process:

1. Give each participant a sheet listing a series of sayings or proverbs from a range of countries (see Attachment for sample but be sure to remove the country identifiers before distributing).
2. Place participants in groups of 3–5 and allow them 10 minutes to answer the following three questions:
   a. What is the message being communicated?
   b. What value could this message be supporting?
   c. What country might this saying be from?
3. Debrief.

Debriefing Questions:

1. What was this experience like?
2. What did you notice? Look for different values demonstrated by different sayings.
3. What implications did you identify?

Debriefing Conclusions:

1. Every culture has sayings or proverbs that communicate cultural values.
2. Using a proverb or saying that others around you don't understand can disrupt effective communication.
3. Understanding sayings or proverbs from other cultures can give you an insight into their cultural values—and can be fun.

Optional way to conduct the exercise:

Instead of providing a list of sayings/proverbs, have each small group of participants generate their own list of sayings they have heard or learned growing up and then respond to the three questions.

Attachment: Cross-Cultural Sayings and Proverbs

1. The nail that sticks up feels the hammer first.—Japan
2. We really need to play hardball.—United States
3. The members are keeping things close to the vest.—United States
4. Put your nose to the grindstone.—United States
5. Fish and visitors smell after three days.—United States
6. To drown in a glass of water.—Mexico
7. Don't make an elephant out of a mosquito.—Estonia
8. The slowest barker is the surest biter.—France
9. The early bird gets the worm.—United States
10. No flies get into a closed mouth.—Mexico
11. Just because you wake up early, the dawn won't happen any sooner.—Mexico
12. The leaves on the tree do not last forever.—Mexico
13. Tell me who you run around with and I will tell you who you are.—Mexico
14. Too much and too little ruins everything.—Sweden
15. Better take what is certain than aim for the uncertain.—Sweden
16. The one who opens his mouth for a lot, often loses the whole piece.—Sweden
17. Very often behind a sweet talking mouth is hiding a poisonous heart.—Romania
18. The truth rises to light as the oil above the water.—Romania
19. The one who is not right is the one who screams louder.—Romania
20. A word is not a sparrow; once it flies out you can't catch it. Russia
21. Heaven is high; Emperor is far.—China

46

Mr. Ramirez or José

Time Required:

45 minutes: 20 minutes activity, 25 minutes debrief

Objectives:

To help participants:

1. Explore formal and informal communication styles.
2. Identify the advantages of each style.
3. Understand the possible impact of using formal and informal communication styles.

Materials:

Formal and Informal Communication Handout (see Attachment)

Chart paper

Markers

Process:

1. Distribute and discuss formal and informal communication handout (the attachment).
2. Have individuals identify their style preference.
3. Divide participants into formal vs. informal preference groups.
4. Have each group work together to answer the following questions:
   a. Where did your style preference originate?
   b. What feelings do you have when someone uses the other style?
   c. What are the advantages of your style? Chart the advantages.
5. Bring the large group back together. Discuss questions a–c.
6. Compare the "advantages" charts.
7. Debrief.

Debriefing Questions:

1. What are some similarities/differences in origination of preference?
2. Was it easy or difficult to identify the advantages of your style?
3. Why might you have strong feelings associated with your preferred style?
4. Were you surprised by any of the "advantages" of the other style?
5. Is it possible to adjust or switch styles? Why or why not?

Debriefing Conclusions:

1. Style preferences are learned early in life.
2. Strong feelings tend to be associated with the preferred style.
3. It tends to be easier to identify the advantages of your preferred style than those of the other style.
4. Both styles have advantages.
5. It is possible to adjust style but you are likely to incur a level of discomfort.

Attachment: Formal and Informal Communication Handout

One factor to be considered in communication styles is the level of formality used in communication. Cultural influences and individual preferences affect how formally or informally we frame our communication. Misunderstandings and miscommunication can occur when the sender and receiver have a different style preference.

Formal Communication

- Status and hierarchy are valued and supported.
- Strict rules apply to the way someone is addressed based upon things such as age, status (personal/professional), gender, specific topic.
- Organizational hierarchy applies to who can/cannot talk to whom and which circumstances allow for direct communication.

Informal Communication

- Equity and fairness are valued and supported
- Few rules apply to the way people are addressed. First names are frequently used.
- Communication is less bound by convention. There is greater latitude in what can be said, to whom one can speak, and under what circumstances one can speak.

© Patricia Cassiday, Ed.D. and Donna Stringer, Ph.D., 2008.

47

Public/Private Self

Time Required:

45 minutes: 5 minute introduction; 5 minutes for self-assessment, 15 minutes in small groups, 20 minutes debrief

Objectives:

To help participants identify:

1. Personal public/private style and the origins of those preferences.
2. How differences in public/private style can affect workplace perceptions and communication.

Materials:

Public/Private Self-Assessment form and Target Handout for each participant

Colored pen or pencil for each participant (see the Attachment)

Process:

1. Briefly point out that different cultures teach different "appropriate" topics for discussion with friends and family or work colleagues. Ask if anyone has an example.
2. Give each participant a Public/Private Self-Assessment form. Ask them to check which topics they would be willing to discuss publicly (with casual acquaintances or in the workplace) or only privately (with close friends or family). Note that the definition of public or private is up to each individual. Explain that once they have completed the assessment, they should count the number of private checks and, beginning with the center circle on the handout, color in as many rings as they have private checks. Allow approximately 5–10 minutes for them to do the test and mark the circle.
3. Place participants in small groups of 3–5 people. Ask them to discuss how their circles are similar or different and what implications this particular personal style has for how we perceive one another at work and how those perceptions can

affect our communication with one another in the workplace. Allow 15 minutes for small group discussion.

4. Ask people to share observations with the large group.

Debriefing Questions:

1. What did you notice as you completed your own assessment?
2. What did you notice as you began discussing the results with your small group? Were there any themes that emerged?
3. What are the potential implications of this style difference in the work environment?

Debriefing Conclusions:

1. Public/private does NOT equate to introvert/extrovert. Someone with a large private self can be quite extroverted, talking a lot but divulging nothing personal; conversely, someone with a very small private self may be very quiet and talk only if someone else initiates the conversation.
2. People with the same size circle are not necessarily compatible; they could have very different topics they are willing to discuss.
3. Very private people may perceive public people as too talkative, foolish, nonprofessional; public persons may see very private people as shy, arrogant, hostile, or stupid.
4. If circumstances occur in which a public person encourages a private person to divulge more than they normally would, it could result in the private person feeling embarrassed, as if they have used bad judgment, or as if they are unnecessarily vulnerable. It is important not to encourage people to share more than they feel is safe.
5. Circles can change with age/experience. As people get older they tend to have smaller circles—fewer things feel risky to them. Conversely, if someone has taken the risk to divulge information and has been "burned," their circle is likely to get larger fast.
6. There is a wide range of cultural differences regarding appropriate conversational topics. For example, money, personal beliefs, political beliefs, and family are inappropriate topics in some places but widely accepted in others. Have participants identify similarities/differences in topics that are considered appropriate for "public" discussions.

Attachment: Public/Private Self-Assessment

Please mark the following topics as

Private: if it is comfortable to discuss only with close friends or family

Public: if it is comfortable to discuss with casual friends or strangers

ATTITUDES AND OPTIONS	Public	Private
What I think and feel about my religion: my personal religious views		
My political views		
My views on racial integration or interracial relationships		
My views on sexual morality		
My views on controversial issues (e.g., immigration, gun control, abortion)		
TASTES AND INTEREST		
What Internet sites I like to visit regularly		
My music preferences		
My favorite reading matter		
Hobbies or experiences I enjoy		
The kind of party or social gathering I like best		
WORK OR STUDIES		
Things I lack in education, skills, or training that will limit my career		
My strongest skills, education, or training that will help me succeed in a career		
My goals and ambitions in my work or career		
How satisfied or unsatisfied I am with my work or career		
How I really feel about the people I work for or with		
FINANCES		
How much I earn: my salary and other sources of income		
Whether I owe money, and how much		
My total financial worth		
My immediate and long term financial goals		
How good I am at managing my money		

PERSONAL ISSUES		
Things I dislike about myself		
Emotions I can/cannot share with others		
Information about my sex life		
Things I would rather my parents had not taught me		
Things I am glad I have learned		
BODY		
How I feel about my physical abilities		
How I feel about my physical appearance		
My feelings about my body: what I would or would not change		
My medical history		
Feelings about my sexual adequacy		
TOTALS		

Developed by Donna Stringer, Ph.D., 2008. Sources: Dean C. Barnlund. (1975). *Public and Private Self in Japan and the United States*. Yarmouth, Maine: Intercultural Press; and Paul Pedersen. (1988). *A Handbook for Developing Multicultural Awareness*. Alexandria, Virginia: American Association of Counseling and Development.

Target Handout

Total the number of marks in the **Private** column on the Public/Private Self-Assessment.

Color in the number of circles, starting from the center, equal to your Private Score.

Developed by Donna Stringer, Ph.D., 2008. Sources: Dean C. Barnlund. (1975). *Public and Private Self in Japan and the United States*. Yarmouth, Maine: Intercultural Press; and Paul Pedersen. (1988). *A Handbook for Developing Multicultural Awareness*. Alexandria, Virginia: American Association of Counseling and Development.

What Do You See?

48

Time Required:

45 minutes: 15 minutes to introduce and review D.I.E., 15 minutes with scenarios, 15 minutes to debrief

WORKPLACE
EDUCETION
VERBAL
M–H

Objectives:

To help participants:

1. Clarify the difference between Description, Interpretation and Evaluation.
2. Explore the influence of cultural and personal experience on perception.
3. Provide practice in generating multiple interpretations for any described behavior.
4. Provide practice in distinguishing between interpretation and evaluation.

Materials:

D.I.E. Handout, one for each participant (Attachment A)

Possible Scenarios, one for each participant (Attachment B)

Process:

1. Introduce and review the D.I.E. Handout (Attachment A).
2. For each scenario (Attachment B), ask participants to generate as many explanations as possible for what is happening here.
3. For each explanation generated for what is happening here, ask participants to evaluate it as good or bad, right or wrong.

Debriefing Questions:

1. What did you find easiest about this exercise? Most difficult? Why?
2. Were any of the scenarios more difficult to work with? Why?
3. How might personal or cultural preferences influence perception of the situation? Examples?

4. What could help you be most accurate in your interpretations?
5. How might you use this in the future?

Debriefing Conclusions:

1. Our interpretations and evaluations of what we see are based on our personal experience and cultural learning.
2. Making a conscious decision to "describe" what we see *first* can help us avoid forming inaccurate conclusions.
3. Asking questions about what is happening can provide clarification.
4. Generating multiple explanations (interpretations) of what we observe is a sign of cultural competence.
5. Evaluations can shift from bad to good or vice versa once we have an accurate interpretation.

Attachment A: Description, Interpretation, Evaluation (D.I.E.) Handout

Miscommunication and misunderstandings occur when the message being sent is different from the message being received. What we hear and how we understand what is being said is filtered through our cultural lens, personal perspective, and individual preferences. Applying the principles of D.I.E., an effective communication tool, can help reduce miscommunication and misunderstandings.

Description

- Describe only what you hear/see.
- Objectively list the facts.
- Do not draw any conclusions.

Interpretation

- Determine what the behavior "means."
- Ask the "actors" what their behavior means from their perspective. This is the best way to avoid misinterpreting intention.
- If you are unable to ask, generating multiple interpretations for the behavior you observe is an effective way to avoid getting locked into a single explanation from your own cultural/ experiential perspective.

Evaluation

- Is the behavior good or bad? Acceptable or unacceptable?

EXAMPLE:

Describe: For our previous three meetings, you arrived later than we agreed to. Help me understand what is happening.

Interpretation: You moved to a new bus route and have had difficulty figuring out what time you need to be at the bus stop to get here on time, but things should get better in the future.

Evaluation: While I don't like the behavior, I can understand it now and am willing to give it another try.

Our interpretation and evaluation of specific behavior is deeply rooted in our personal experience and cultural perspective. When we observe a behavior, we may think we know or understand the meaning, but without asking about the intent, we may be way off base. Organizations and individuals interested in developing greater cultural competence will benefit from using the D.I.E. approach.

Attachment B: Possible Scenarios

A group of European men are in a local coffee shop. Everyone is gathered around a small table. Voices are raised. Some men stand and one man pounds the table top.

A man and woman are standing at the street corner. The man is standing some distance from the woman. He is speaking. She is looking down.

A group of teenage girls are gathered outside of a fast-food restaurant. Everyone seems to be talking at once. Several girls are laughing.

Three women wearing scarves are standing outside of the library. One woman is wiping tears from her face. One woman is talking to her. The third woman is looking up and down the street.

One man is sitting at his desk. The other man is standing over the desk pointing and talking loudly.

In the elevator a mother and her teenage daughter are standing some distance apart and the mother is repeating the daughter's name.

A young couple is sitting close together on a park bench. She is laughing and he looks very serious. He seems to be leading the conversation.

A group from your office is gathered in the hallway. Everyone stops talking as you approach the group.

The airline ticket agent is talking to the woman ahead of you. Suddenly the woman puts her head down and begins to sob.

You enter the doctor's office. Several people in the waiting room are talking loudly and quickly. Everyone looks up as you enter the room.

© Patricia Cassiday, Ed.D. and Donna Stringer, Ph.D., 2008.

Delivering the Message

49

Time Required:

90 minutes: 15 minutes to introduce presentation style information and create teams, 15 minutes preparation, 40 minutes for four presentations with feedback, 20 minutes to debrief

Objectives:

To help participants:

1. Explore communication preferences.
2. Plan presentations designed for a diverse audience.
3. Increase flexibility and adaptability in presentation design.

Materials:

Presentation topics on index cards (Attachment A)

1 Presentation checklist per person per presentation (Attachment B)

Communication Preferences handout (Attachment C)

Pencils/pens

Process:

1. Provide an introduction regarding several communication style preferences (Attachment C).
2. Divide participants into groups of 4–5.
3. Ask each team to draw a presentation topic.
4. Give teams 15 minutes to prepare a 5 minute presentation and select a member to make their presentation.
5. Before presentations, distribute the Presentation Checklists.
6. After each team presentation, allow five minutes for the group to provide feedback from the Presentation Checklists, focusing on any changes the group feels would improve communication with the intended audience.
7. Debrief in large group

Debriefing Questions:

1. How did you feel about the assignment? Your group interaction?
2. Were there style differences within your group? How did those differences affect the way you decided to approach your presentation?
3. What special considerations went into your presentation design?
4. Which style preferences are easiest for you to incorporate? More difficult? Why?
5. How could you use this information in the future?

Debriefing Conclusions:

1. Everyone has preferences in communication style.
2. Organizations have preferred presentation styles.
3. Presentations can be strengthened by utilizing cultural insights regarding communication style preferences.
4. Incorporating various style preferences when addressing a diverse audience can improve communication.

Attachment A: Presentation Topics

You are a U.S.–based project management team for a cosmetic company. Your new product line will be manufactured in France. You are presenting to the newly formed French project team.

Your organization has a plant in California and one in Mexico. Due to a decline in profits, your company has announced employee layoffs are eminent. You are the Human Resource management team, presenting information on the most prudent reduction points.

Your training team has been asked to present a team-building seminar for auto workers in Kansas. The team is composed of U.S. and Japanese auto workers. Your goal is to enhance productivity by building team confidence and cooperation.

The city council in your local home town plans to build a new corrections facility. Your team has been asked to present a building design and budget for this project.

You designate a current topic relevant to your organization

Attachment B: Presentation Checklist

As you listen to each presentation, identify which of the following elements the presentation contains. Be prepared to discuss whether these elements might be the most effective for the intended audience.

Introduction:

_____ Brief and direct
_____ References to expertise, authority
_____ Designed to build connection

Process:

_____ Formal
_____ Informal
_____ Objective data
_____ Subjective information
_____ Direct/specific
_____ Indirect/diplomatic
_____ Intellectually challenging
_____ Specific justifications
_____ Expert approach/top-down
_____ Group participation/consensus

Closing

_____ Presents an action plan
_____ Seeks agreement from the audience
_____ Verifies concepts
_____ Plans for next steps
_____ Recognizes group effort

Attachment C: Communication Preferences: Considerations for Presentation Design

Both individuals and groups (cultures) have preferences for how they receive information. Communication can be provided and received in several of the following ways. The more closely the presentation style matches the audience's communication and learning preferences, the more effective will be the communication. These style issues should be considered when designing and making presentations:

Does your intended audience prefer to receive information in a:

- Linear, objective, "thinking" approach
- Subtle, personalized, "feeling" approach
- Factual, logical, data driven approach
- Manner that uses examples, metaphors, stories
- Direct manner with clear, brief statements
- Indirect manner with stories, metaphors
- Informal manner with the audience involved; speaker may sit or walk around the room
- Formal manner with presentation material and speaker-driven; speaker standing in the front of the room
- Manner that allows open discussion with disagreement minimized
- Manner that allows open discussion with disagreement expressed openly
- Manner that allows decisions based on facts and results
- Manner that allows decisions based on impact on people, relationships, and morale
- Manner that offers information orally, without visual material
- Manner that offers information orally, with visual material

50

The "Right" Fit

WORKPLACE
VERBAL
M–H

Time Required:

95 minutes: **Round 1** 20 minutes for activity, 20 minutes debrief; **Round 2** 15 minutes introduction, 20 minutes activity, and 20 minutes debrief

Objectives:

To help participants:

1. To communicate clarity in job descriptions.
2. To identify "differences that make a difference" in interview behaviors and personal preferences for work styles.
3. To develop interview strategies for finding the "right" fit.

Materials:

Copies of recent job announcements

Handout: Does the Difference Make a Difference? (Attachment A)

Personal Preferences: Considerations for Organizational Assignments checklist (Attachment B)

Process:

ROUND 1: JOB DESCRIPTION

1. Divide participants into teams of 4–5.
2. Give each team a recent job announcement from the organization.
3. Ask teams to answer the following questions:
   a. Does the job title accurately describe its purpose?
   b. Are the job responsibilities clearly defined?
   c. Are the expectations specific? Measurable/quantifiable?
   d. Are the behavioral expectations clearly defined? What are the actual behaviors you want the person to exhibit? For example, it might say "Must be a team player." What does

it mean to be a team player in your organization? In some organizations a team-player:

- works closely with others, builds consensus, and comes to agreement before taking action.
- has expertise, uses respectful confrontation, argues, pushes back to generate more diverse and/or creative solutions.
- makes decisions and takes independent action to facilitate the team process, creating the latitude needed for the team to function.

ROUND 2: INTERVIEWING PROCESS

1. Continue in teams or whole group.
2. Discuss the "Does the Difference Make a Difference?" handout.
3. Ask participants to answer the following questions using the interview checklist:
   a. Is this a difference that makes a difference in our organization?
   b. Under what circumstance could this make a difference? Not make a difference?

Remind participants to make decisions within an organizational and cultural context, such as, "direct eye contact" (in relation to a specific position). Not making direct eye contact might be a problem for the receptionist position but no problem for an accountant role.

Debriefing Questions:

1. What did you think or learn while reviewing the job description?
2. Which interviewing considerations were most applicable to your organization?
3. Was it difficult or easy deciding on which differences made a difference? Why?
4. Which differences are easiest for you to incorporate? More difficult? Why?
5. How could you use this information in the future?

Debriefing Conclusions:

1. Organizations often look for "best fit" in candidates without a clear examination of what it means, and what types of candidates might be unintentionally excluded.
2. Clarity of communication is enhanced by consideration of organizational and cultural context.
3. An organization's ability to attract a diverse cross-cultural workforce is enhanced by utilizing clear communication in job descriptions and in interviews.

4. The use of clear, unambiguous language in a job description can promote the attraction of "best qualified" candidates.

5. Identifying behaviors that do or do not make a difference can avoid unintentionally eliminating a candidate whose behaviors are different from the organization's norms but do not make a difference in performance of job requirements.

Attachment A: Does the Difference Make a Difference?

Our interpretation and evaluation of specific behavior is deeply rooted in our personal experience and cultural perspective. When we observe a behavior, we may think we know or understand the meaning, but without asking about the intent, we may be way off base. Organizations interested in developing a diverse, multicultural workforce need a broader understanding of behavior within a cultural context. Once we understand what the behavior means within the cultural context, we can decide if the difference is something that would make a difference in our organization.

Here are four places where the difference does make a difference in the workplace:

1. The behavior reduces productivity or effectiveness with people.
2. The behavior threatens legality, including organizational policies and procedures.
3. The behavior is unsafe.
4. The behavior increases cost to the organization.

If a behavior does not affect any of these things, it is not a difference that makes a difference. In organizations committed to diversity, it is important to encourage understanding and acceptance of difference: allowing someone to behave in his or her own manner when it does not impact any of the four areas above.

If the behavior does make a difference, identify how you are going to tell the individual that the behavior must be modified in this workplace, or for this position.

Note: Telling someone a behavior does not work in this organization—because it is a difference that makes a difference—does not mean the behavior is bad or wrong in all contexts. Asking that a behavior stop for one of the above-listed four reasons need not be a negative judgment—only an evaluation in relationship to a specific workplace.

Attachment B: Personal Preferences: Considerations for Organizational Assignments

Under what circumstances would these behaviors make a difference in our organization? In relation to a specific position?

Personal Preferences:

_____ Work independently
_____ Work with others

_____ Orderly, quiet work environment
_____ Active, stimulating environment

_____ Solve the customer's problem
_____ Provide information so the customer can solve his/her own problem

_____ One task at a time
_____ Multitasking

_____ Predictable rules, structure
_____ Flexibility, rules open to interpretation

_____ Enjoy working with those similar to self
_____ Enjoy working with multicultural teams

_____ Prefer working in harmony
_____ Comfortable with conflict

_____ Preference for status quo
_____ Comfortable with change

BEHAVIORAL CONSIDERATIONS

- Eye contact
- Appearance/style/dress
- Speaking with an accent
- Comfort with informality or formality
- Direct vs. indirect communication style
- Ability to talk about one's self in an interview

© Patricia Cassiday, Ed.D. and Donna Stringer, Ph.D., 2008.

"Meeting" Your Needs

51

Time Required:

60 minutes: 5 minutes to set up, 15 minutes for small group activity, 20 minutes for four team presentations, 20 minutes to debrief

Objectives:

To help participants:

1. To explore planning, scheduling, and facilitating a meeting.
2. To increase flexibility and adaptability in meeting design.
3. To identify components of meetings that are useful for enhancing communication/effectiveness.

Materials:

1 Meeting Checklist for each participant (Attachment A)

Meeting scenarios (Attachment B)

Pencils/pens

Process:

1. Distribute and review the Meeting Checklist.
2. Divide participants into groups of 4–5 and give each team a meeting scenario.
3. Give teams 15 minutes to prepare a 5 minute presentation answering the following questions:

    How and what will you communicate:

    Before the meeting?

    During the meeting?

    After the meeting?

4. Ask each team to select one member to deliver the presentation to the large group.
5. Debrief.

WORKPLACE

VERBAL

NONVERBAL

L

Debriefing Questions:

1. What challenges, if any, did your team experience?
2. Did style difference or technology expertise play a role in your plan?
3. What are some of the greatest communication challenges related to meetings in your organization?
4. How could you use this information in the future to reduce those challenges?

Debriefing Conclusions:

1. Effective communication can enhance participant involvement in meetings.
2. Awareness of style preferences can improve meeting effectiveness.
3. Considering cultural and individual style preferences when planning meetings facilitates effective communication for diverse participants.

Attachment A: Meeting Checklist

The following items all involve communication between meeting planners and attendees. They also can facilitate effectiveness if the planner is aware of cross-cultural implications in each of the following areas.

Logistics:

- Date, time, location. For example, open and frequent communication can avoid disadvantaging certain individuals because of location—virtual meetings being held at 9 AM in New York means someone around the globe may be meeting at 10 PM; Saturday meetings may exclude Jewish employees; early meetings may exclude those with childcare issues, and so on.
- Agenda: who sets it and how? Before the meeting or at the meeting?
- Face-to-face or virtual?
- Equipment needed
- Seating arrangement
- 100 percent attendance required? Acceptable percentage? Substitutes?
- Length
- Other

Purpose / Design:

- Information sharing. For example, does all information flow from "top down" or is each individual at the meeting expected to provide some information?
- What level of participation is expected during the meeting of attendees?
- Facilitation style
- Problem solving
- Decision making
- Team building
- Product planning
- Policy development
- Other

Outcomes:

- Action plan. For example, does the group decide what needs to be done and agree as to who will do what, or is it important that the "leader" make all task assignments?
- Responsibilities: who and by when?
- Product
- Policy/Regulation
- Plan for next steps
- Other

Attachment B: Meeting Scenarios

1. You are to conduct a meeting with a curriculum design team. The members of the team know each other well. They are located in Bangkok, Johannesburg, Frankfurt, Dublin, New York, and San Francisco. The purpose of the meeting is to outline broad categories of training activities. These activities, including all necessary materials, are due to the client in 30 days.

2. You are to meet with a health care organization for the first time. This meeting will be with the Human Resource team. Members of the team know each other well. Twelve people will be on site and one person will be available by teleconference. The purpose of the meeting is for you to provide a 30 minute cross-cultural training, followed by a facilitated discussion of how this information can be disseminated throughout the organization.

3. You are scheduled to facilitate a one day meeting in Houston. The group attending is a recently reconfigured sales team. Members of the group are currently located in Mexico City, New York, and San Francisco. The team members have not met prior to this meeting. The purpose of the meeting is to agree upon responsibilities for the newly defined regions.

You designate a scenario relevant to your organization at this time.

52

How Rude Was That?

Time Required:

30–40 minutes: 15–20 minutes for activity and 15–20 minutes to debrief

WORKPLACE
EDUCATION
VERBAL
L

Objectives:

To help participate:

1. Explore cultural concepts related to politeness.
2. Discuss behavior that could be considered rude in different cultures.
3. Understand the possible cross-cultural impact of "polite" behavior.
4. Practice taking the perspective of the "other."

Materials:

How Rude Was That? Worksheet (Attachment A)

Pencils or pens

Process:

1. Ask participants to complete the "rudeness" worksheet.
2. Form dyads and/or triads to share responses to the worksheet.
3. Ask discussion questions:
   a. Which answers were the same? Different?
   b. How can meanings change within different cultural contexts?
   c. How might this affect the way you perceive the other person? The way you communicate with that person?
   d. Are there any behaviors you consider rude that are not on the checklist that you would like a different perspective or interpretation for?

Debriefing Questions:

1. Who or what determines the rules for politeness? Where do we learn it?

2. Were there any surprises about what can be considered rude? Acceptable? Describe them.
3. Where might these behaviors cause the greatest misunderstanding?
4. How might you use this information in the future?

Debriefing Conclusions:

1. Appropriate behavior in one culture may be considered rude in another culture. It all depends on the cultural context.
2. It is important to ask for more information about what we experience or observe, especially if we are offended by the behavior or don't understand it.
3. Our opinion of people can be influenced by our perception of their behavior.
4. Our opinion, whether positive or negative, can affect how we communicate in an ongoing manner with that individual.

Attachment A: How Rude Was That? Worksheet

For each item below check "Yes" if you would consider the behavior rude or inappropriate. Check "No" if the behavior would be considered acceptable.

1. Asking how much you paid for your car   _____ Yes   _____ No

2. Burping at the end of a meal   _____ Yes   _____ No

3. Avoiding eye contact during a conversation   _____ Yes   _____ No

4. Sharing personal health information   _____ Yes   _____ No

5. Arriving late for a meeting with no explanation   _____ Yes   _____ No

6. Asking why someone does not have children   _____ Yes   _____ No

7. Telling the details of a friend's divorce   _____ Yes   _____ No

8. Remarking about an obvious weight gain   _____ Yes   _____ No

9. Using a toothpick at the dinner table   _____ Yes   _____ No

10. Eavesdropping on a conversation   _____ Yes   _____ No

11. Offering no recognition for someone who helped you   _____ Yes   _____ No

12. Looking right at the person when speaking   _____ Yes   _____ No

13. Bringing your dog into a restaurant   _____ Yes   _____ No

14. Presenting a thank-you gift to a coworker   _____ Yes   _____ No

15. Kissing in public   _____ Yes   _____ No

16. Arriving early and "pitching in"   _____ Yes   _____ No

17. Telling someone they do not look well   _____ Yes   _____ No

18. Not assigning specific seats at the table   _____ Yes   _____ No

19. Calling someone by their first name   _____ Yes   _____ No

20. Spitting on the sidewalk   _____ Yes   _____ No

Some Core Techniques for Improving Cross-Cultural Communication

1. *Be aware of your own biases* so they don't unconsciously control your behaviors. Research indicates that *merely being reminded that we have biases* will allow decisions to be made in a more bias-free manner.

2. *Practice flexibility.* The more choice you have in the different ways you can communicate, the more effective you will be in a cross-cultural context. Consider three important aspects of communication competence:
   - *Understand your own preferences* in style and process.
   - *Allow others to communicate in a range of ways*—without negative evaluation.
   - *Use a wide range of styles and processes* depending on context.

3. *Slow down your response* and *check your assumptions.* Many organizations operate at a very fast pace—and, in fact, reward quick responses. When this is added to a conscious or unconscious assumption that we are more like others than unlike them, it can lead to a quick response based on assumptions. When this quick reaction is based on an inaccurate assumption, it reduces cross-cultural effectiveness. Asking ourselves "what assumptions am I making?" and "how do I know my assumption is accurate?" allows us the opportunity to be more effective.

4. *Assume positive intentions.* When people say or do things that have a negative impact on us, we may assume they meant to do so. It is our experience, however, that most people mean well most of the time—negative impact on others is frequently the result of assuming that we are "all alike" and do things with good intentions that are simply misunderstood. Assuming that someone else has positive intentions will allow us to begin a conversation both to discover their intent and to share the impact of their behavior on us. If their intention was positive, they will be more likely to behave in ways that we appreciate

based on the feedback we have given them. This fits with another technique, which is to:

5. *Share the impact* of other's behaviors on you—and ask them to do the same.

6. *State your intent.* Negative communication impacts often occur because the sender of a message assumes that the receiver of the message will understand their positive intent. When communicating across cultural differences, however, this is not a safe assumption. Telling someone your intention helps avoid this misunderstanding.

7. *Listen with TING*—listen openly and empathically. This is key to effective communication—and especially cross-cultural communication.

8. Use the process of *Describe, Interpret, Evaluate (D.I.E.)* when someone else's behaviors are confusing to you—or you don't like them. This is a great technique for better cross-cultural communication.

9. Ask of someone else's behavior, "*Is a difference that makes a difference?*" This is an advanced technique, made possible only when someone is able to set aside their own behavioral preferences and consider how another behavior might work. If someone else's behavior does not negatively affect (a) cost; (b) people or productivity; (c) safety; or (d) legality, then it is not generally a difference that makes a difference, and allowing someone to use behaviors that are most culturally comfortable for them will increase their feelings of being respected.

General Classification of Activities

Activity #	Title	Context and Type	Communication Themes	Risk Level	Time Required
1	Communication Continuum Exercise	Workplace Education Verbal	Style Differences	L–M	60 Min.
2	Second Language Walk-in-Their-Shoes	Workplace Education Verbal	Second Language	L	20 Min.
3	Decoding "Work Speak"	Workplace Verbal	Seeking to Understand Conflict	M–H	30 Min.
4	Alpha-Beta Partnership	Workplace Verbal Nonverbal	Negotiation Conflict Seeking to Understand	M–H	60 Min.
5	A Fair Shake	Workplace Education Verbal Nonverbal	Greetings	L	20–30 Min.
6	The Language of Gestures	Workplace Education Nonverbal	Gestures	L	30–45 Min.
7	Rational, Emotive, Intuitive	Workplace Education Verbal	Style Differences	L–M	60 Min.
8	What Would You Do?	Workplace Education Verbal	Style Differences	M	45–60 Min.
9	How Would I Say That?	Workplace Education Verbal	Style Differences	M	60 Min.

Activity #	Title	Context and Type	Communication Themes	Risk Level	Time Required
10	E-mail: Communicating Across Culture	Workplace Higher Education Verbal Written	Style Differences	M	60–90 Min.
11	Toothpicks	Workplace Education Nonverbal	Style Differences	L–M	45–60 Min.
12	Building Cultural Bridges to Communication	Workplace Nonverbal Written	Style Differences	M–H	90–120 Min.
13	Are You Listening?	Workplace Education Verbal Nonverbal	Style Differences	L–M	40–50 Min.
14	Communicating Policy in a Cultural Context	Workplace Education Written	Style Differences	M	30–45 Min.
15	Can Anyone Hear Me?	Workplace Education Verbal	Team Processes	L–M	50–60 Min.
16	Communication Solutions	Workplace Verbal Nonverbal	Decision Making Conflict	M–H	100–120 Min.
17	Persuasion	Workplace Verbal	Decision Making Conflict	H	30–60 Min.
18	My Rule/Your Rule	Workplace Education Verbal Nonverbal	Seeking to Understand	M–H	60 Min.
19	Thought Bubble Role-Plays	Education Workplace Verbal Nonverbal	Seeking to Understand Conflict	L–M	60 Min.
20	Different Days— Different Ways	Education Workplace Verbal Behavioral	Seeking to Understand	M–H	60 Min.
21	Building Team Communication	Workplace Verbal	Style Differences	L–M	90 Min.

Activity #	Title	Context and Type	Communication Themes	Risk Level	Time Required
22	Bridging Behaviors	Workplace Education Verbal	Seeking to Understand	M–H	45 Min.
23	The Intercultural Classroom	Higher Education Workplace Verbal Nonverbal	Style Differences	M–H	90 Min.
24	What's in a Word?	Workplace Education Verbal Nonverbal	Seeking to Understand	L–M	45 Min.
25	Pacing	Workplace Education Nonverbal	Style Differences	L	30 Min.
26	Switching Directions: Direct/Indirect	Workplace Education Verbal Nonverbal	Style Differences	M	45 Min.
27	Your Choice: Style Continuum	Workplace Education Verbal	Style Differences	M–H	80–100 Min.
28	Debate or Dialogue?	Workplace Verbal	Conflict Negotiation	M–H	90–120 Min
29	First Impressions	Workplace Education Verbal Nonverbal	Icebreaker Greetings	L	35–45 Min.
30	Sounds Like Silence	Workplace Education Verbal Nonverbal	Style Differences	L–M	40–60 Min.
31	Me, Myself, and E-mail	Workplace Education Nonverbal Written	Style Differences	L–M	50 Min.
32	High Road, Low Road	Workplace Education Verbal Nonverbal	Style Differences	L–M	45 Min.

Activity #	Title	Context and Type	Communication Themes	Risk Level	Time Required
33	E-mail Intent vs. Impact	Workplace Nonverbal	Style Differences	L	45 Min.
34	Be Specific!	Workplace Verbal	Seeking to Understand	L–M	30 Min.
35	My Inner Rules	Workplace Nonverbal	Self-Awareness	M–H	60 Min.
36	Nondefensive Communication	Workplace Verbal Nonverbal	Self-Awareness Seeking to Understand	M–H	80 Min.
37	My Name Is . . .	Workplace Education Verbal	Seeking to Understand	M	60 Min.
38	PALS Dialogue	Workplace Education Verbal	Seeking to Understand Conflict	M–H	100 Min.
39	If I Woke up Tomorrow . . .	Workplace Verbal	Seeking to Understand	H	105 Min.
40	Building Style Proficiency	Workplace Education Verbal	Style Differences	M–H	60 Min.
41	Build a Structure	Workplace Education Nonverbal	Style Differences Seeking to Understand	M	45 Min.
42	Talking Through Touch	Workplace Education Nonverbal	Style Differences Clarify Meaning	M–H	45 Min.
43	He Learned She Learned	Workplace Higher Education Verbal Nonverbal	Self-Awareness Gender	L–M	45 Min.
44	I Think—You Feel	Workplace Verbal	Style Differences	M–H	65 Min.
45	What a Funny Thing to Say!	Workplace Education Nonverbal	Icebreaker Seeking to Understand	L	30 Min.

Activity #	Title	Context and Type	Communication Themes	Risk Level	Time Required
46	Mr. Ramirez or José	Workplace Education Verbal Nonverbal	Self-Awareness Seeking to Understand	L	45 Min.
47	Public/Private Self	Workplace Education Nonverbal	Self-Awareness	L	45 Min.
48	What Do You See?	Workplace Education Verbal	Seeking to Understand	M–H	45 Min.
49	Delivering the Message	Workplace Verbal	Style Differences	M–H	90 Min.
50	The "Right" Fit	Workplace Verbal Nonverbal	Seeking to Understand	M–H	95 Min.
51	"Meeting" Your Needs	Workplace Verbal Nonverbal	Seeking to Understand	L	60 Min.
52	How Rude Was That?	Workplace Education Verbal	Seeking to Understand	L	30–40 Min.

References

Adler, Nancy. (1986). "Communicating Across Cultural Barriers," Chapter 3 in N. Adler, *International dimensions of organizational behavior.* Boston, MA: Kent Publishing.

Barna, LaRay. (1997). "Stumbling blocks in intercultural communication." In L. A. Samovar and R. E. Porter (Eds.), *Intercultural communication: A reader, 8th edition.* Belmont, CA: Wadsworth.

Barnlund, D. C. (1975). *Public and private self in Japan and the United States.* Yarmouth, ME: Intercultural Press.

Bennett, J. M. (1993). Cultural marginality: Identity issues in intercultural training. In M. Paige (Ed.), *Education for intercultural experiences* (pp. 1–27). Yarmouth, ME: Intercultural Press.

Bennett, J. M. (1998). Transition shock: Putting culture shock in perspective. In M. J. Bennett (Ed.), *Basic concepts of intercultural communication: Selected readings* (pp. 215–223). Yarmouth, ME: Intercultural Press.

Bennett, M. J. (Ed.). (1998). *Basic concepts of intercultural communication: Selected readings.* Yarmouth, ME: Intercultural Press.

Brislin, R., and Yoshida, T. (1994). *Intercultural communication training: An introduction.* Thousand Oaks, CA: Sage Publications.

Casse, P. (1981). *Training for the cross-cultural mind* (2nd ed.). Washington, DC: SIETAR.

Cassiday, P. A. (2003). "Leadership in International Settings: Exploring the Values, Beliefs and Assumptions of Expatriates." Unpublished doctoral dissertation, Seattle University, Seattle, WA.

Condon, J. C., and Yousef, F. (1975). *An introduction to intercultural communication.* New York: MacMillan.

Cooperrider, D. L., Sorensen, P. F., Whitney, D., and Yaeger, T. F. (Eds.). (2000). *Appreciative inquiry: Rethinking human organization toward a positive theory of change.* Champaign, IL: Stripes Publishing.

Cox, T. H. (1993). *Cultural diversity in organizations: Theory, research and practice.* San Francisco: Berrett-Koehler Publishers.

Cox, T. H., and Blake, S. (1991). Managing cultural diversity: Implications for organizational competitiveness. *Academy of Management Executive, 5*(3), 45–56.

Cox, T. H., and McLeod, P. (1991). Effects of ethnic group cultural differences on cooperative and competitive behavior on group task. *Academy of Management Executive, 34*(4), 827–847.

Eberhardt, L. Y. (1995). *Bridging the gender gap.* Duluth, MN: Whole Person Associates.

Elashmawi, F., and Harris, P. R. (1998). *Multicultural management 2000: Essential cultural insights for global business success.* Houston, TX: Gulf Publishing.

Gardenswartz, L., Digh, P., and Bennett, M. (2003). *The global diversity desk reference: Managing, an international workforce.* San Francisco: Pfeiffer and Co.

Gardenswartz, L., and Rowe, A. (1994). *Diverse teams at work: Capitalizing on the power of diversity.* New York: McGraw-Hill.

Goldstein, S. (2008). *Cross-cultural explorations: activities in culture and psychology* (2nd ed.). Boston, MA: Pearson Education.

Gudykunst, W. B. (1991). *Bridging differences: Intergroup interaction.* Newbury Park, CA: Sage Publications.

Hall, E. T. (1959). *The silent language.* New York: Doubleday.

Hall, E. T. (1966). *The hidden dimension.* New York: Doubleday.

Hammer, M. R. (1987). Behavioral dimensions of intercultural effectiveness: A replication and extension. *International Journal for Intercultural Relations, 2,* 65–88.

Haslett, B. (1989). Communication and language acquisition within a cultural context. In S. Ting-Toomey and F. Korzenny, (Eds.), *Language, Communication, and Culture.* Newbury Park, CA: Sage Publications.

Herrell, A. L. (2007). *Fifty strategies for teaching English language learners.* Upper Saddle River, NJ: Corwin Press.

Hofstede, G. (1997). *Culture and organizations software of the mind: Intercultural cooperation and its importance for survival.* New York: McGraw-Hill.

Isaacs, W. (1999). *Dialogue.* New York: Random House.

Jandt, F. E. *An introduction to intercultural communication: Identities in a global community.* Thousand Oaks, CA: Sage Publications.

Kim, Y. Y. (1991). Intercultural communication competence: A systems-theoretical view. In S. K. Ting-Toomey (Ed.), *Cross-cultural interpersonal communication.* Newbury Park, CA: Sage Publications.

Kolb, D. A. (1985). *LSI learning style inventory: Self-scoring inventory and interpretation booklet.* Boston: McBer and Company.

Kolb, D. A., and D. M. Smith. (1985). *User's guide for the learning style inventory.* Boston: McBer and Company.

Leslie, J. B., and VanVelsor, E. (1998). *A cross-national comparison of effective leadership and teamwork: Toward a global workforce.* Greensboro, NC: Center for Creative Leadership.

Martin, J. N., and Nakayama, T. K. (2000). *Intercultural communication in contexts* (2nd ed.). Mountain View, CA: Mayfield Publishing.

Mindess, A. (1999). *Reading between the signs: Intercultural communication for sign language interpreters.* Yarmouth, ME: Intercultural Press.

Nessel, D. D. (2008). *Using the language experience approach with English learners: Strategies for engaging students and developing literacy.* Thousand Oaks, CA: Corwin Press.

Norales, F. O. (2006). *Cross-cultural communication: Concepts, cases and challenges.* Youngstown, NY: Cambria Press.

Paige, R. M. (Ed.). (1993). *Education for the intercultural experience* (2nd ed.). Yarmouth, ME: Intercultural Press.

Pedersen, P. B. (2000). *A handbook for developing multicultural awareness.* Alexandria, VA: American Counseling Association.

Pedersen, P. B. (2004). *110 Experiences for multicultural learning.* Washington, DC: American Psychological Association.

Pusch, M. D., and Wurzel, J. (1999). "Foundations of Intercultural Communication." Paper presented at the Summer Institute for Intercultural Communication, Forest Grove, OR.

Ramsey, S. (1988). "To hear one and understand ten: Nonverbal behavior in Japan." In L. A. Samovar, and R. E. Porter, (Eds.), *Intercultural communication: A reader.* Belmont, CA: Wadsworth.

Reyes, S. A., and Vallone, T. L. (2007). *Constructivist strategies for teaching English language learners.* Thousand Oaks, CA: Corwin Press.

Reynolds, S., and Valentine, D. (2004). *Guide to cross-cultural communication.* Upper Saddle River, NJ: Pearson Education.

Rosen, R., Digh, P., Singer, M., and Phillips, C. (2000). *Global literacies: Lessons on business leadership and national cultures.* New York: Simon and Schuster.

Ruderman, M. N., Hughes-Jones, M. W., and Jackson, S. E. (1996). *Selected research on work team diversity.* Greensboro, NC: Center for Creative Leadership.

Samovar, L. A., and R. E. Porter (Eds.). (1997). *Intercultural Communication: A reader,* 8th ed. Belmont, CA: Wadsworth.

Saphiere, D. H., Mikk, B. K., and DeVries. (2005). *Communication highwire: Leveraging the power of diverse communication styles.* Boston, MA: Intercultural Press.

Schein, E. H. (1985). *Organizational culture and leadership.* San Francisco: Jossey-Bass.

Schein, E. H. (1999). *Corporate culture: Survival guide.* San Francisco: Jossey-Bass.

Seelye, H. N. (1996). *Experiential activities for intercultural learning* (Vol. 1). Yarmouth, ME: Intercultural Press.

Seelye, H. N., and Seelye-James, A. (1996). *Cultural clash: Managing in a multicultural world.* Lincolnwood, IL: NTC Publishing Group.

Segall, M. H., Dasen, P. R., Berry, J. W., and Poortinga, Y. H. (1999). *Human behavior in global perspective: An introduction to cross-cultural psychology* (2nd ed.). Needham Heights, MA: Allyn and Bacon.

Senge, P. M. (1990). *The fifth discipline: The art and practice of the learning organization.* New York: Doubleday.

Senge, P. M. (1999). *The dance of change.* New York: Doubleday.

Simons, G. F., Vasquez, C., and Harris, P. R. (1993). *Transcultural leadership: Empowering the diverse workforce.* Houston, TX: Gulf Publishing.

Stewart, E. C., and Bennett, M. J. (1991). *American cultural patterns: A cross-cultural perspective.* Yarmouth, ME: Intercultural Press.

Storti, C. (1994). *Cross-cultural dialogues: 74 Brief encounters with cultural difference.* Yarmouth, ME: Intercultural Press.

Stringer, D. M., and Cassiday, P. A. (2003). *52 Activities for exploring values differences*. Yarmouth, ME: Intercultural Press.

Thiagarajan, S. (2000). *Interactive experiential strategies for multicultural learning*. Portland, OR: Summer Institute for Intercultural Communication.

Thiagarajan, S. (2006). *Thiagi's 100 favorite games*. San Francisco: John Wiley and Sons.

Ting-Toomey, S. (1999). *Communication across cultures*. New York: Guilford Press.

Triandis, H. C. (1972). *The analysis of subjective culture*. New York: Wiley.

Trompennaars, F., and Hampden-Turner, C. (1998). *Riding the waves of culture: Understanding diversity in global business*. New York: McGraw-Hill.

VanVelsor, E., and Leslie, J. B. (1995). Why executives derail: Perspectives across time and culture. *Academy of Management Executive, 9*(4), 62–72.

Varner, I., and Beamer, L. (1995). *Intercultural communication in the global workplace*. Boston: McGraw Hill.

Weeks, W. H., Pedersen, P. B., and Brislin, R. W. (1977). *A manual of structured experiences for cross-cultural learning*. Yarmouth, ME: Intercultural Press.

Wells, T. (1980). *Keeping your cool under fire: Communicating non-defensively*. New York: McGraw Hill.

Wilson, M. S., Hoppes, M. H., and Sayles, L. R. (1996). *Managing across cultures: A learning framework*. Greensboro, NC: Center for Creative Leadership.

Wiseman, R. L., Hammer, M. R., and Nishida, H. (1989). Predictors of intercultural communication competence. *International Journal for Intercultural Relations, 13*, 349–370.